The Demolition
of Skid Row

The Demolition of Skid Row

Ronald J. Miller
Chadron State College

LexingtonBooks
D.C. Heath and Company
Lexington, Massachusetts
Toronto

Library of Congress Cataloging in Publication Data

Miller, Ronald J.
   The demolition of skid row.

   Bibliography: p.
   Includes index.
   1. Skid row—United States—Case studies.   2. Tramps—Services for—
United States.   I.   Title.
HV4505.M53   305.5'6   81-47182
ISBN 0-669-04563-2   AACR2

Copyright © 1982 by D.C. Heath and Company

Published simultaneously in Canada

Printed in the United States of America

International Standard Book Number: 0-669-04563-2

Library of Congress Catalog Card Number: 81-47182

To my mother,
Harriet Roby Miller

and my father,
the late Glenn Wilcox Miller

Contents

List of Figure and Tables   ix

Acknowledgment   xi

Chapter 1   **They Are Running the Bums out of Town**   1

Skid Row as an Urban Neighborhood   2
Skid Row as a Way of Life   3
Apologia   6
Skid Row as a Social Problem   8
The Natural Decline of Skid Row   13
Urban Renewal: Strategy, Opposition,
    and Interests   15
Social-Welfare Policy on Skid Row   16
Skid Row Revival?   20
Seattle's Skid Road as a Case Study   22
Conclusion   25

Chapter 2   **Where Do the Dogs Bark?**   27

The Theoretical Vista   27
Conclusion   42

Chapter 3   **Documenting in Loving Detail**   47

The Skid Row–ness Scale   47
Police Department Data   55
Census Data   56
Detox   56
Skid Row Interviews   57
Potters Field Burials   58
A Similar Effort   58
Conclusion   59

Chapter 4   **Not Dice**   61

Street Data   62
Police Data   76
Medical Examiner's Records   81

                        Census Data   82
                        Detox   90
                        Street Questionnaire   92
                        Conclusion   92

Chapter 5   Convincing Citizens, Politicians, and Other
                        Scientists   95

                        Data Review   95
                        Policy Implications   100
                        Solutions   103
                        Critique   104

Chapter 6   One of the Paths   107

Appendix A   Street-Data Limitations   125

Appendix B   Common Names of Areas in Seattle and
                        Corresponding Seattle Police Department and
                        U.S. Census Bureau Numeric Designations   129

Appendix C   U.S. Census Bureau Data Sources, Table
                        Names, and Page Numbers   131

                        References   133

                        Index   141

                        About the Author   148

List of Figure
and Tables

Figure

6-1   Northwest United States and Selected Railroad Towns   109

Tables

2-1   Summaries of Theories and Their Predictions of
           Skid Row Location Following Dispersal   43

2-2   Cumulation of Hypotheses   45

3-1   The Skid Row-ness Scale and Ratings of the
           Centrality of Each Scale Item to Skid Row   48

4-1   Street-Observation Areas, Sizes, and Locations   63

4-2   Grand-Total Skid Row-ness Scores, by Year and
           Area, with Percentages of Yearly Totals and
           Proportions of 1972 Scores   64

4-3   Institutional-Item Total Scores, by Year and Area,
           with Percentages of Yearly Totals and Proportions
           of 1972 Scores   66

4-4   Transitory-Item Total Scores, by Year and Area, with
           Percentages of Yearly Totals and Proportions of 1972
           Scores   68

4-5   Observations of Derelicts, by Area and Year, with
           Percentages of Yearly Totals and Proportions of
           1972 Observations   71

4-6   Observations of Loiterers, by Area and Year, with
           Percentages of Yearly Totals and Proportions of
           1972 Observations   72

4-7   Observations of Discarded Bottles, by Area and Year,
           with Percentages of Yearly Totals and Proportions of
           1972 Observations   73

4–8   Grand-Total Skid Row–ness Scores of
        Special-Category Blocks, by Year, with Percentages of
        Yearly Totals and Proportions of 1972 Scores   75

4–9   Arrests for Typical Skid Row Offenses, by Year and
        Census Tract, Including Percentage of Total Such
        Arrests and Proportion of Such Arrests Occurring
        in December, January, and February   77

4–10   Number of Charges Preferred in Typical Skid
        Row–Area Arrests and Their Respective Percentages
        of all Arrests   80

4–11   Areas of Home Address of People Who Died in
        Seattle between 1 July 1971 and 30 June 1972 and
        between 1 July 1977 and 30 June 1978 with No
        Known Living Relatives   83

4–12   Demographic Data Pertinent to Skid Row–ness, by
        Area and Year   86

A–1   Street-Observation Block Coverage and Skid
        Row–ness Scores Recorded in the Years 1972 through
        1977 on the Blocks Covered in 1978   126

B–1   Common Names of Areas in Seattle and
        Corresponding Seattle Police Department and U.S.
        Census Bureau Numeric Designations   129

C–1   U.S. Census Bureau Data Sources, Table Names, and
        Page Numbers   131

Acknowledgment

While several people contributed toward the progress and completion of this book, only one suggested, prodded, and encouraged from beginning to end. For that, my deepest appreciation goes to my mentor and friend, Professor Armand L. Mauss. The Seattle Urban Research Station of the Washington State University Sociology Department, supported for four years by the National Science Foundation, was an invaluable resource in the early years of this book's preparation.

1

They Are Running the Bums Out of Town

Larimer Square

The bulldozer's rollin' through my part of town.
The iron ball swings and knocks it all down.
You knocked down the flophouse, knocked down the bars,
And blacktopped it over to park all your cars.

Chorus
Now, where will I go and where can I stay
When you've knocked down the Skid Row and hauled it away?
I'll flag a fast rattler and ride it on down, boys.
They're runnin' the bums out of town.

Old Maxie the tailor is closing his doors.
There ain't nothin' left in the secondhand stores.
You knocked down the hock shop and the big Harbor Light,
And the old Chinese cafe that was open all night.

Well, you ran out the hookers who worked on the street.
And you built a big club where the playboys can meet.
My bookie joint closed when your cops pulled a raid,
But you built a new hall for the stock market trade.

These little storekeepers just don't stand a chance
With the big uptown bankers a callin' the dance.
With their suit-and-tie restaurants that're all owned
  by Greeks,
And the counterfeit hippies and their plastic boutiques.

Now I'm finding out there's just one kind of war,
The one going on 'tween the rich and the poor.
I don't know a lot about what you'd call class,
But the upper and middle can all kiss my ass.

—Bruce (Utah) Phillips

Larimer Square was the heart of the Skid Row in Denver. In virtually every city in the United States, most of the buildings that served the sector of soci-

ety living in what is known as "Skid Row" have been demolished or renovated. This large-scale attack on what is usually the oldest residential and
commercial section of downtown areas is a very recent phenomenon. Social
conditions and population composition in these areas have been relatively
stable for nearly a century (Wallace 1965) with only periodic minor shifts in
location and periodic increases and decreases in population size corresponding to business recessions and booms and to the seasonal demands of railroad building and maintenance, agriculture, and lumbering. The question
of the location of Skid Row—its institutions, people, and characteristic
behavior patterns following the recent onslaught—is the topic of this study.

Skid Row as an Urban Neighborhood

The name *Skid Row* evolved from the term *skid road* which originally
referred to a structure on which logs were skidded down a hill to a sawmill
in Seattle, Washington. The taverns, cheap hotels, and bordellos that bor-
dered the log skid outlived the skid itself but retained the name (Morgan
1960). A skid road was any road or path, especially a built-up one, used by
loggers to move logs, especially downhill (Vanderkooi 1973). As the term
Skid Road came to describe comparable business areas in other cities, it
became *Skid Row,* implying the bottom of a downward path of social
mobility, "the skids," and the limited geographical area in which persons in
such circumstances find themselves, "the row." The downward path most
often has been from youth, health, hope, and a series of unskilled temporary jobs to age, discouragement, layoffs, and wine drinking (Wallace
1965).

Modern descriptions of Skid Row areas vary but are on the whole quite
consistent. Wiseman writes

> To the average person, the term *Skid Row* immediately brings to mind a
> grey, slumlike section of town peopled with society's misfits and castoffs,
> poverty-stricken men who have failed to make it in the competitive world
> and are now eking out an existence in an alcoholic haze amid environmen-
> tal squalor and human misery. [1970, p. 3]

Bogue writes that Skid Row is

> [A] concentration of substandard hotels . . . intermingled with numerous
> taverns, employment agencies offering jobs to unskilled laborers, restau-
> rants serving low-cost meals, pawnshops and secondhand stores, and mis-
> sions that daily provide a free meal after the service. Perhaps there are also
> barber colleges, burlesque shows or nightclubs with striptease acts, penny
> arcades, tatoo palaces, stores selling men's work clothing, bakeries selling
> stale bread, and unclaimed freight stores. [1963, p. 1]

Caplow (1970) identifies the historical constituents of Skid Row as vagrants, chronic inebriates, seasonal laborers, retired manual laborers, unaffiliated steadily emloyed men, and in smaller proportions, fugitives, cripples, the temporarily unemployed, soldiers, petty criminals, and even a few women.

Skid Row in the past was not much different than now except there was more action. No longer can one see "more than 1,000 prostitutes within an area of five blocks" (Black 1926, p. 33). More money was controlled by Skid Row men in the past than today. The numbers of migrant and temporary workers and the importance of their work were greater in an economy that ran more on labor than machines. "Hobohemia" of Chicago in the early 1920s had all the institutions of the present-day Skid Row and more:

> West Madison, being a port of homeless men, has its own characteristic institutions and professions. The bootlegger is at home here; the dope peddler hunts and finds here his victims; here the professional gambler plies his trade and the "jack roller," as he is commonly called, the man who robs his fellows while they are drunk or asleep; these and others of their kind find in the anonymity of this changing population the freedom and security that only the crowded city offers.

> The street has its share also of peddlers, beggars, cripples, and old, broken men; men worn out with the adventure and vicissitudes of life on the road. One of its most striking characteristics is the almost complete absence of women and children; it is the most completely womanless and childless of all the city areas. It is quite definitely a man's street. [Anderson 1923, p. 5]

Health statistics (Bogue 1963; Wiseman 1970; Blumberg, Shipley, and Shandler 1973) usually show Skid Row to be the area of the city in which most afflictions occur most often. Fire statistics show clearly that Skid Row is a high-risk area (Bogue 1963; Blumberg, Shipley, and Shandler 1973). Skid Row lodging is also among the worst in the United States.

Skid Row as a Way of Life

While some authors focus on the characteristics of the area in general, the majority of Skid Row researchers deal primarily with the life-style of Skid Row men and the subculture of skid row (Bahr 1970). Extensive literature focuses on the transient, sometime habitués of Skid Row—hoboes and tramps—and their traveling experiences. Some of these studies note that most of those living in a Skid Row area are not wino-derelicts. Bahr (1973; 1974) finds that many men who share the Skid Row characteristics of disaffiliation, poverty, and physical defects are not drinkers at all. Many more are not problem drinkers. Often implied, however, is that it is the longstanding, visible subculture of drinking residents and transients that gives Skid Row its name and much of its common reputation. Allsop quotes a hobo:

> When you've got a gallon of wine you feel happy for a few hours, but it's a sewer; it's a dirty, pointless life. You have no friends, only drinking acquaintances who, same as you, are frightened, discouraged men. You're in a rut, stuck in the mud.
>
> You say, "Let's go to Tucson, Arizona; let's go to New York to look at the World's Fair; let's go up to Seattle," but you take your troubles with you from state to state. It's a life of a thousand jails and a thousand flophouses. All the time, wherever you go, you got your own Skid Row right there inside your head. [1967, p. 24]

Caplow (1970, p. 5) lists the major components of Skid Row life-styles as isolation from women, wine drinking, free disposition of one's time, and absence of compulsory obligations toward others.

Alcohol is a central part of the lives of a large number of men on Skid Row, through definitely not all, and the pattern of drinking involves sharing liquor rather than the alcoholic pattern of surreptitious drinking. Wiseman (1970, pp. 14–16) reports that in the opinion of those she interviewed, life is seen more optimistically in relatively perpetual drunkenness than when one is sober.

Wiseman (1970) further reports that a today or now orientation was an obvious part of the Skid Row drinker's mental framework. Orwell (1933, p. 20) observes this same orientation but attributes it instead to poverty: "When you are approaching poverty, you make one discovery which outweighs some of the others. You . . . discover the great redeeming feature of poverty: the fact that it annihilates the future."

Three other personality characteristics are found by Wiseman in the ideal Skid Row–type man: (1) a feeling of powerlessness coupled with a sense of need for cunning to outwit a hostile and unfair world; (2) an adjustment to an acceptance of impermanence—socially, monetarily, and residentially; and (3) a mixture of extreme independence from others coupled with acceptance of dependence from time to time. Anderson (1923, pp. 261–262) writes of the hoboes of his time but could be taken as assessing a characteristic of the subculture that more or less lives on: "The hobo, in his songs and in conversation, shows unmistakably his aversion to all efforts to remake his character or reshape his destiny."

Bahr agrees somewhat with Blumberg, Shipley, and Moor's (1971) assessment that the differences between Skid Row–like people and other residents of the so-called natural area of Skid Row are slight, but he makes an important distinction that very nicely describes an essential quality of the life-style and the neighborhood of Skid Row:

The Skid Row people live on Skid Row territory; the others do not. In terms of the ecology of the city, the concentration of institutions and persons with homeless characteristics creates a neighborhood, a context, which is different from other regions of the city, both in terms of symbolic nature (how people think about it, treat its residents, and relate to it) and in terms of population composition. Skid Row may reflect a state of mind, but it is also a place, an area of the city, and those who frequent it are aware of its distinctive identity. [Bahr 1973, p. 35]

Degradation is a dominant feature of life on Skid Row, not only in relation to the distinctive identity Skid Row has in the minds of the general population but also, or especially, in the contacts some Skid Row men have on Skid Row. Spradley (1972) describes the pattern of contact betwen Skid Row men and the police as unfair, cruel, and pointless. He identifies fifteen distinct stages of processing in the passage of the public inebriate on the street-police-court-jail-street route, taken over and over again by homeless men. Each step has degrading aspects, implied by Spradley to cause a negative self-concept formation among bums. Most degrading of all for Spradley is the fact that if one has $20 to post bond, the whole procedure, sometimes including a six-month sentence, is avoidable.

The missions on Skid Row are important, sometimes degrading institutions serving nearly all Skid Row men at least occasionally. Wallace (1965) dates the efforts of the missions among homeless men as early as 1801 in this country. Christian religion is thematic in the services of virtually all of these missions, though some nonreligious organizations operate otherwise as missions do—that is, providing food, clothing, shelter, and employment. Not all missions provide all of these, however. The relationship between Skid Row men and the missions is and apparently always has been the opposite of mutual respect (Anderson 1923; Harris 1961; Wiseman 1970). One has to sing for one's supper. In most missions, partaking of refreshments following the service requires that one participate at least passively in almost the entire service without causing a disturbance. Doors are sometimes locked after a certain point in the service to insure that no one will enter late (Wallace 1965). Preachers know they have sinners before them, and they hold back little in proclaiming it. Men causing a disturbance, sometimes audible and sometimes not, are reprimanded and are occasionally literally thrown out the door by assistants, usually former Skid Row men who work and live at the mission. Men who habitually frequent missions, especially if they live in one, are known as "mission stiffs," and their role is of extremely low status among Skid Row men (Anderson 1923; Wallace 1965). Wallace (1965, p. 50) writes that mission attenders sense the missions are as dependent on them as they are on the missions. Bogue (1963, p. 250) does identify a recreational function missions fulfill—something to do in the evening—but on Skid Row, missions usually are seen as temporary sources of bed and board.

Historically, this perspective is cleverly evident in a poem by Kemp (1914, p. 60) entitled "Tramp Confession." Reprinted in Anderson (1923, pp. 196–198), this long poem tells of a cold winter night near the end of a mission service. A tramp, thinking of the bitter wind outside, comes forward to the call for sinners. After much praying, and his repenting, he is given a bed. Later, alone in prayer, he asks Jesus forgiveness for his lie.

Skid Row is a complex set of interrelations as is any other role set with thousands of characters. It has its hierarchy of status and reward, and as in any other setting there are ups and downs in fortune for participants. With the median status so low, the downs on Skid Row can be very discouraging. For example, the suicide rate is high (Blumberg, Shipley, and Shandler 1973).

Apologia *[Sociologists fascinated with hobos here]*

Why the lives and conditions of men at the very bottom of the status hierarchy should be a continuing theme in sociological research is no small puzzle. Caplow (1970) writes that every field has its certain fascinating topics. Hamlet is such a topic for literary scholars. The fruitfly occupies this position in genetics. Skid Row similarly occupies sociologists. Bahr writes

> There is probably no other type of problem area in the United States about which we are as well informed as Skid Row. In what other area do we have solid empirical data going back nearly continuously for eighty years? Indeed, we must admit that the extent of our information is disproportionate to the number of persons involved or the urgency of the problem. [1974, p. 11]

Bahr (1974) provides a brief review of major Skid Row studies, from McCook's (1893) "Tramp Census," through Nascher's (1909) *The Wretches of Povertyville,* Rice's (1918) "The Homeless," Anderson's (1923) *The Hobo* and (1940) *Men on the Move,* Sutherland and Locke's (1936) *Twenty Thousand Homeless Men,* up to modern studies stimulated by the federal urban-renewal program. Bahr (1970) has also compiled an extensive annotated bibliography dealing with the Skid Row man and his counterparts in different countries and over several centuries. Studies of Skid Row continue even after much of the former physical habitat of the subculture has been destroyed or renovated.

Various observations can be adduced for temporal continuity of such studies. The early pattern of studying social problems and the accompanying reformist, meliorative tradition in sociology provide still the underlying rationale for some Skid Row studies. Knowing more about Skid Row may help determine the best policy for handling the problem. In the 1920s, Skid Row took on human-ecology significance as part of a zone in the flow of ecological processes described and documented especially in the efforts of Chicago sociologists. Anderson's *The Hobo* immortalized the subculture. Currently, studies of deviance and social problems include focus on the alcoholic in various settings, and Skid Row is a characteristic and visible setting of alcohol consumption. Also, it is one of the easiest subcultures to study because very few difficult barriers to admission exist.

Caplow, in puzzling over the question of why sociologists study Skid Row, concludes it is because Skid Row men are so different:

> Whatever else he may be, the Skid Row man is not his brother's keeper. Nor his brother's opinion leader, norm enforcer, or action initiator—that is to say, he is about as different from *Homo Sociologus* [emphasis Caplow's] as it is possible to be while still remaining human. Therein lies Skid Row's fascination for the sociologist. For the price of a subway ride, he can enter a country where the accepted principles of social interaction do not apply. [1970, p. 6]

Subtler factors may also be related to the focus on Skid Row life. Considerations of audience appeal no doubt prompt most city newspapers to feature Skid Row characters at least once every few years in a major story with photographs and brief life histories. These stories almost always point out the squalor of Skid Row conditions. Consider one article, for example, entitled "The Hole" (Powers 1980). The lurid subtitle reads, "Deep under the Streets of New York There Is another World—A World Where the Hobos Dwell." Most writers, however, including Powers (1980), find some color or romanticism in the lives of Skid Row men. The abject circumstances featured may give readers pause to count their blessings and may have some propriety-maintenance function by showing the consequences of irresolute behavior. The romantic aspect, the Skid Row man's luxury of freedom, may touch deeper. Freud, in *Civilization and Its Discontents* (1930), made the point that something in the psyche of every civilized person is chafed by the loss of individual freedom that social life necessarily entails. Vicarious experience of the Skid Row life of freedom perhaps mollifies this loss.

Some sociological researchers and others find Skid Row subjects fascinating as quasi members of society who have broken many of the bonds with which society holds us. Some sociologists, however, imbued with knowledge of social organization and process, approach what is on the surface a disorganized, disheveled bunch of social dropouts and delight in demonstrating that most aspects of social life—norms, sanctions, stratification, roles, and definition of the situation—are present in this seemingly structureless subculture.

At the least, through study of Skid Row we may be entertained by colorful characters, and perhaps we may feel better about our own state in life. Better, we may extend our awareness of humanity to another sector and sympathize if not empathize with a deprived group. We hope ultimately through this study to develop a significant overall understanding of social behavior.

Skid Row as a Social Problem

If Skid Row has been an object of fascination among sociologists, other sectors of society have not treated it so kindly. Historically, a number of interest groups have done battle with different aspects of Skid Row. Mauss (1975) has developed a typology of interest groups and has explored social movements as the labeling of certain conditions as problematic by these interest groups. The interest groups Mauss identified are economic, political, occupational, moral, psychological, and scientific. Skid Row has especially attracted the ire of economic, moral, and political interests as well as apparently purely aesthetic interests.

Historic Political Opposition

The hoboes of the Skid Row of old were associated with, or at least exposed to, the influence of the International Workers of the World (IWW) (Anderson 1923; Allsop 1967), a fundamental Marxist group (Rooney 1970) regularly involved in labor organizing and violence, usually initiated by concerned citizens. Anderson (1923) describes the antipathy that settled, small-town folks had, not only for the IWW but for other hoboes, tramps, and bums. Sheriffs and/or posses sometimes made mean work of cleaning up a "jungle," or hobo camp. Persecution was a typical strategy, especially when the work the hoboes came for was done.

Historic Economic Interests and the Legal Strategy

Fending off the so-called knights of the road was probably not usually inspired by political differences. The men were reputed to be thieves, and they certainly did beg. Then, and now, various towns and cities have acquired the reputation among tramps of being tough, and the reputations are usually not accidentally earned. Violence and jailing are strategies to maintain a low transient population. Information about various local enforcement policies comprises a significant part of communication sought and given in extended conversations common to these men. For a transient or local man to ignore such data could mean a stint at unpaid labor—jail crews work for nothing.

Writer and hobo Spradley (1970) recalls being before a Milwaukee judge for public intoxication. He sensed the judge's displeasure when told that the man before him was from Minneapolis, a city where the major Skid Row had recently been completely rebuilt in an urban-renewal project. The judge had noted a marked influx of Skid Rowers from that city, and Spradley got a maximum sentence. This typical punitive orientation has probably seldom, if ever, been effective in reducing the numbers of Skid Row men in a city for more than a short while, but less-punitive strategies do even less.

Local courts have a way of assuring the departure of undesirables. The term *time hanging* refers to the additional sentence a person can count on receiving if apprehended again in the locale. Unfortunately for each locale, nearly every other locale uses the same tactic.

Moral Interests and the Prohibition Movement

No small effort to eliminate Skid Row, or at least much of its atmosphere, was Prohibition. Drinking was roundly condemned on moral grounds. The following quote from an annual report on the American Temperance Society conveys the tone of the campaign:

> Ardent spirit destroys the soul. To use it is an immorality, a violation of the will of God. . . . The use of ardent spirits tends strongly to hinder the moral and spiritual illumination of men and thus to prevent their salvation. [Asbury 1950, p. 40]

While antiliquor interests did not confine themselves to Skid Row establishments, these establishments gave much impetus to Prohibition. The low state to which taverns on Skid Row had dropped was one of the issues that caught the sentiments of a sufficient proportion of the population to make alcoholic beverages illegal (Asbury 1950).

Early antiliquor advocates were not taken seriously either by brewers and distillers or the general public. Carry Nation, in her hatchet-swinging, bottle-breaking, keg-smashing days, was a comical news feature. Brewers facetiously invited her to smash more taverns for the publicity her antics generated, but the moral tide of teetotalism gained strength until the American Congressional Temperance Society was established. Following shortly, many state congressional societies developed, and Massachusetts was the first to form one (Asbury 1950, p. 35). Righteous songs were taught to school children by the Women's Christian Temperance Union, and the degenerate effects of alcohol were declaimed in lecture and pamphlet across the country by members of the Anti-Saloon League. The Anti-Saloon League was foremost in the drive that led to the Eighteenth Amendment (McCarthy 1949, pp. 32–33). They were well organized with state programs directed through a national board of directors. Voluntary contributions from the wealthy and a system of pledges in churches financed league activities. This nonpartisan league backed sympathizers running for office and entered campaigns against individuals known to favor the alcoholic-beverage industry (McCarthy 1949, pp. 32–33). This social movement culminated in 1920 with the Eighteenth Amendment, which forbade the sale of alcohol for internal consumption.

The effect of Prohibition on Skid Row was to close the "barrel houses" where men drank great quantities of alcohol and were free to spend the night on the floor. The Eighteenth Amendment probably reduced the quantity of liquor consumed on Skid Row considerably. Anderson (1923) makes no lengthy topic of liquor in his work that covered other aspects of Skid Row in great depth. However, Prohibition did not stop Skid Row drinking altogether. Prohibition may have developed ties between organized crime and Skid Row because of the position of organized crime in supplying alcohol. Although the average Skid Row drinker may have been as low class in the organized-crime status hierarchy as he was in the legitimate-opportunity structure, no doubt homeless men were drawn into illegal roles. The special vocabulary of hoboes that Anderson (1923) identified overlaps with gangster or criminal vocabulary—for example, "gun moll" (dangerous woman) or "yegg" (roving desperado). Collier and Somfay (1974) give a glossary of Skid Row argot used in their text, and they include the terms "con artist," "fink," and "mark," among others, that are related to criminals or criminal action. Bogue (1963, pp. 65–68) reports on criminals on Skid Row and makes a distinction between Skid Row and criminal worlds. Bogue writes that "it is usually only petty criminals who flee to Skid Row to hide out or live on Skid Row and use it as a regular base of operations."

Business Interests and Action

Proprietors of businesses in the vicinity of Skid Row perhaps have felt most personally financially touched by the problem of Skid Row men. The presence of these men probably does restrict clientele. While the Skid Row trade has been the mainstay of some establishments, respectable business owners and managers at best view Skid Row askance. The following examples not only display the scope of commercial efforts to curb Skid Row but also provide a view of the social conditions that have kept Skid Row men mobile. For example, the Bowery in New York has weathered spirited campaigns designed to contribute to its downfall. The Manhattan East Side Chamber of Commerce in 1946 initiated a program designed to "clear the streets of chronic drunkards" (*The New York Times* 1946). They went so far as to propose to the city council changing the name of the Bowery to change its image (*The New York Times* 1947). In 1953, the same organization and a group known as the Outdoor Cleanliness Association proposed different tactics aimed at the Bowery, including denial of rehabilitation services to chronic drunks, removal of a local welfare station, and investigation of the paint-supply business to cut off supplies of varnish and cheap alcohol to derelicts (*The New York Times* 1953).

Contemporary Plans and Rationale for Eliminating Skid Row

While historical efforts to curb, contain, or drive away aspects of Skid Row have been unsuccessful on a long-term basis, a more-contemporary, combined approach appears to be more efficacious in defining, managing, and reducing Skid Row as a social problem. In 1959, Bogue (1963, pp. 475–476) submitted a plan to the city of Chicago that, if carried out, would have eliminated that city's Skid Row in five years. He identified virtually every type of person who might live on Skid Row as "problem cases" and provided rationale for their removal and steps by which this could be accomplished. Skid Row, Bogue argued, was dying of its own lack of a viable economic base. Hotels were half empty. Taverns were closing. Skid Row had changed from an economic asset to an economic liability, with police, fire, and other city service costs' exceeding the railroad and other paychecks spent in Chicago. Bogue maintained that the proportion of the casual-labor market occupied by Skid Row men could easily be made up by others. Bogue argued also that development opportunities are lost because Skid Row poisons a broad surrounding zone. Similar economic arguments for the elimination of Skid Rows were made by Nimmer (1972) and Plaut (1967).

Bogue's (1963:478–496) 1959 prototype program of elimination contained twelve steps:

1. Dispose of Skid Row housing in two phases, an immediate "shrinking" and a final phaseout as housing is provided for the elderly, indigent, and erstwhile Skid Row residents on a quite different plane.
2. Institutionalize mentally ill, seriously ill, and senile.
3. Care for dependent elderly, and housing for working men who are not alcoholics.
4. Provide medical rehabilitation for disabled.
5. Provide occupational training.

6. Institute a program for alcoholics who are not willing to cooperate voluntarily or who refuse to be helped by AA or the missions.
7. Provide sheltered employment.
8. Provide rehabilitation for ex-cons.
9. Formulate a plan for the detection and management of parasites.
10. Institute a program for the rehousing and possible socialization of asocial, antisocial, and semineurotic persons who prefer to live in isolation.
11. Institute a program to eliminate exploitation.
12. Institute a program of preventive action with special emphasis upon dealing with newcomers to Skid Row.

This early plan, essentially to demolish the area and flood the residents with wanted or unwanted services, was not alone. Plunkert (1961) suggested that if our society really wished to end Skid Row as a social problem it could be done. For this task Plunkert proposed a most comprehensive method, marshalling the skills of those in the fields of internal medicine, psychiatry, psychology, social work, sociology, and religion in an effort that would revolve around a Skid Row diagnostic center staffed by the welfare department in close cooperation with the police.

Plaut also suggests that:

> The total elimination of most Skid Rows—or at least a great reduction in the number of people living under such conditions—may be possible now with the full cooperation of numerous agencies and increased community willingness to tackle basic problems rather than mere symptoms. This objective requires federal funds as a stimulus. [1967, p. 14]

Plaut (1967, p. 115) goes on to identify eleven major services required by homeless persons, including medical screening, hospital and outpatient care, and short-term free shelter and inexpensive lodgings as well as daytime shelter and recreational facilities. Plaut also listed rehabilitation camps and semicustodial and custodial facilities, psychological and social assistance, vocational training and placement, and protective settings such as halfway houses. Such a network of multipurpose services, Plaut argues, would "abolish the ineffective police/legal system of handling public drunkenness." Plaut also writes that another positive outcome of elimination or even a sizable reduction of the Skid Row population would be to help undermine a long-standing public misconception—namely, that the Skid Row bum is the typical problem drinker.

Another argument for the elimination of Skid Rows points out that studies of the criminal-justice system invariably identify understaffing and overextended caseloads (Nimmer 1972). This argument made a good case when combined with the fact that a great proportion (up to 50 percent in some cities) of all arrests involve public drunkenness and that most of those involve Skid Row men (Wallace 1965; Bogue 1963; Wiseman 1970; Pastor 1978). Essentially, the plan as outlined by Bogue and other early strategists was to raze the buildings of Skid Row and flood the residents with social services while relocating them. Action along these lines has indeed proceeded, though not nearly as rapidly as early planners suggested. Urban-renewal programs began on a germinal basis in the 1950s, and social services became a feature of urban life with the war on poverty in the 1960s.

The Natural Decline of Skid Row

While earlier local and issue-specific plans failed to significantly dent Skid Row, later plans on a nationwide scale—namely, urban renewal and social services—have been effective in part because Skid Row was declining of natural or social-structure causes as well. Bogue (1963) argued that the time was ripe for his plan because of this. He cited several forces working against the continuing existence of Skid Row, including the following:

1. The rising level of living in the general population [makes] continued tolerance of the Skid Row situation appear increasingly callous.
2. The rising level of education and urbanization of the population [makes] victims of circumstance—no matter how destitute—discontented and rebellious at having to accept the Skid Row way of life. Rooming-house and hotel proprietors have found they must offer more and better services if they want to keep their clients.
3. A changed public attitude toward alcoholism makes it the subject of public-health and welfare efforts.
4. The gradual humanization of industry has made ruthless hiring and firing of casual employees less frequently the routine way of doing business.
5. Labor offices discriminate against Skid Row men.

Factors that Bahr (1967) identified as responsible for the decline of the Bowery in New York were economic growth, welfare department policy changes inducing men to live elsewhere, and population-composition changes. Jobs became abundant in the 1960s, leaving mostly unemployable men who were preyed upon by muggers. The pensioners and single working-men moved out.

Bahr contacted official informants in forty cities, twenty-four of whom responded that their city's Skid Row area was decreasing in size or population. Only the Skid Row in Tacoma, Washington, was growing. Three were reported to be stable, and officials in twelve other cities did not respond.

Rooney (1970) writes that Skid Row seems to be on the decline and losing much of its character, the economic function it maintained when the single, mobile, workingman was a more-significant feature in the labor market. Rooney writes that:

> If present trends continue, the population of Skid Row will continue to decline, and the proportion of physically disabled Skid Row men will increase. Consequently, Skid Row may come to function as an open asylum. [1970, p. 34]

A comparison of modern and older population estimates of Skid Rows indicates a definite decrease, as does comparison of census-tract characteristics. Anderson, referring to several surveys of lodging houses and hotels, indicates that:

> The number of homeless men in Chicago ranges from 30,000 in good times to 75,000 in hard times. We may say that approximately one-third of these are permanent residents of the city. The other two-thirds are here today and gone tomorrow. When work is plentiful they seldom linger in the city more than a week at a time. In winter when jobs are scarce, and it takes courage to face the inclement weather, the visits to town lengthen to three weeks and a month. From 300,000 to 500,000 of these migratory men pass through the city during the course of a normal year. [1923, p. 3]

VanderKooi (1973) reports that the Chicago Skid Row has a population of 12,000 but does not identify the season in which the population was counted. Rubington (1971), also failing to identify the season, writes that the Bowery population was 15,000 in 1900 and 75,000 in 1919. Bahr's (1974, p. 47) winter Bowery population figures for modern times show a drop in population from 13,675 in 1949 to 6,938 in 1963 with a steady decline to 4,152 by 1972. Lee (1978a) finds that Skid Rows in the West dropped in size most rapidly in the 1960s and that those in the East experienced the greatest percentage decline in the 1950s. Overall, Lee found a decline between 1950 and 1970 of over 50 percent in Skid Row characteristics using census data and Bogue's (1963) definition of Skid Row.

How much of the decline is attributable to changes in population composition and occupational structure rather than social-policy implementation is a complex empirical question. Urban renewal, just by virtue of the nature of its activities, certainly accounts for some of the decline measured by Lee (1978a). If single-room-occupancy hotels are demolished in an area, the proportion of single-room occupancy, one of Lee's measures, will decrease, and that decrease will show up in census data. Lee is currently examining the correlation between urban-renewal expenditures and the proportion of decrease in Skid Row characteristics.

Urban Renewal: Strategy, Opposition, and Interests

Congress enacted the Urban Renewal Program in 1949, and under the auspices of this act, federal authorities, either by negotiation or by using the power of eminent domain, acquire land designated to be cleared. This land can be sold, leased, donated, or retained by the local renewal agency. Housing was the original focus of the Urban Renewal Program of the Department of Housing and Urban Development (HUD). A stated purpose of this organization is the elimination and prevention of slums. The largest proportion of urban-renewal investments has been in purchase of property adjacent to the central business district (CBD). Redevelopment has consisted primarily of commercial facilities, office buildings, and expensive high-rise apartments (Greer 1965). A Toledo, Ohio, urban-renewal official contacted in 1974 reported that to the best of his knowledge this pattern to a large degree had continued since 1965 on a national scale. Bahr (1967) wrote that cities across the country were demolishing low-rent housing and replacing it with luxury apartments and office buildings and that this move was forcing the gradual disappearance of Skid Row.

Another aspect of urban renewal was relocation, finding housing for individuals, and assisting in the relocation of businesses (Greer 1965). The relocation efforts of urban renewal appeared to Anderson (1966) to have been totally inadequate. Many people were simply not relocated, just evicted. Of those who were relocated, many could not or did not stay where they were placed. Wiseman (1970, p. 7) cites part of the publicity campaign of the Pacific City Urban Redevelopment program as illustrating "the mental connection between blighted buildings and blighted individuals in the minds of professional agents of social control." The effort to move men out of the Pacific City Skid Row hotels, which were to be replaced by a sports arena, included a pamphlet designed to suggest that residents apply to the agency for relocation before their hotel was demolished. The pamphlet quoted the highly unfavorable health, fire, and crime statistics of the Skid Row area and then in bold print announced, **"We Say You Deserve Better, Much Better!"**

Anderson(1966), in an article graphically entitled "The Federal Bulldozer," criticizes urban renewal as an unconstitutional violation of private-property rights by the federal government. He points out contradictions to the 1954 Supreme Court ruling that use of eminent domain is proper because urban-renewal land acquisitions are in the public interest. The Supreme Court failed, Anderson argues, to define "public interest."

Anderson also objected because urban renewal destroys good housing and does not improve the living conditions of those displaced. Anderson notes that urban renewal is often disastrous for displaced businesses and, contrary to popular belief, does not necessarily increase taxes paid. Anderson maintains that private enterprise rather than government funds should have been the vehicle for slum clearance. Anderson's critic, Groberg (1966), points out that the government program is not, as Anderson assumes, in competition with private enterprise but rather is in complete cooperation with business leaders and city officials in every city in which it is active. In other words, local interests received federal money and federal bargaining power to clean up Skid Row.

Wallace (1971, p. 448) writes that prior to the passage of the Federal Housing Act of 1949, the law that created urban renewal, two interest groups that had been at odds since the 1930s were temporarily united. The two groups were varied business interests and social-welfare interests. From the perspective of each, urban renewal appeared useful and desirable. According to Wallace, the goals of city planners, architects, engineers, bankers, realtors, and social workers had to be reduced to a common denominator to arrive at the Federal Housing Act of 1949.

Urban-renewal funding has not been the only thing that has cleaned up Skid Row. Historically minded entrepreneurs have created fashionable entertainment, dining, and shopping areas where Skid Row once stood. Art galleries, boutiques, hip taverns, antique stores, and many other businesses are often designed in the style of the period in which the former Skid Row buildings they occupy were erected. However, whether private or urban-renewal action, the effect has been marked and consistent for Skid Rows in cities large and small across the United States—that is, they are physically gone as large, distinct urban areas.

Social-Welfare Policy on Skid Row

Somewhat after the first waves of urban renewal and the private clean up of Skid Row housing, social-welfare-policy changes toward Skid Row became evident. According to Berton (1967), this change occurred in the mid-1960s when the trend in most large cities' clean-up operations on Skid Row was away from jailing drunks in favor of rehabilitation programs. Dating the beginning of service agencies' (other than missions and isolated exceptions) large-scale work with Skid Row men as special-target clientele, Manos (1975) describes the Manhattan Bowery Project on its eighth anniversary, 27 November 1975, as a "graybeard among the programs for public inebriates.'' Shandler (1975, p. 50) observed the Skid Row social-service movement in full swing. He reported that the nation displayed an atmosphere of change, a sense of concern, and an apparent willingness to attack the public-inebriate problem with the interest and support of three federal departments.

The Uniform Alcoholism and Intoxication Treatment Act

The 1971 Uniform Alcoholism and Intoxication Treatment Act (hereinafter, the Uniform Act), primarily a federal recommendation for uniform state policies (Fagan and Mauss 1978), embodies some features of the early plans for cleaning up Skid Row with social services. Basically, the act removes the management of public inebriates from the jurisdiction of the legal system and mandates a continuum of care for problematic alcohol consumers. About twenty states have put the essence of the Uniform Act into law (Fagan and Mauss 1978).

Several observations can be made about the efficiency of the Uniform Act where it has been implemented. The argument that the criminal-justice system would be greatly relieved is only true in part. Fagan and Mauss (1978) aptly point out that releasing police from the duty of picking up drunks does not change their other duties in relation to Skid Row men. They found that drunkenness is often merely the change preferred when, on whatever charge, a police officer acting to keep the peace is bent on getting a man off the street. Some men who would have been picked up on a public-drunkenness charge in the past are now picked up on other charges, following implementation of the Uniform Act. Police in some jurisdictions where the Uniform Act is in force still pick up drunks and escort them to detoxification facilities.

This continued police participation in Skid Row–inebriate treatment is seen by Nimmer (1972) as detrimental to the rehabilitation goal of Skid Row programs for two reasons. First, since the arrest practice is administratively controlled, the men picked up will not form a rational treatment group—that is, only certain types and a limited number are suitable for treatment programs. Second, handling public inebriates can become a very low-priority police duty. In Washington, D.C., for example, public inebriates were required to participate in a three-day maximum-detoxification program with police-initiated contact. Police contacts under the detoxification scheme totaled less than one-tenth of the arrest rates prior to the introduction of the new system. This lower level of contact meant that men were being left on the street.

The Revolving Door

If the Uniform Act can loosely be traced to early plans to clean up Skid Row, then its success appears to be marginal if not negative. The police, degrading as they were, did provide the Skid Row man with temporary room and board. In the cases of many Skid Row men who were repeatedly arrested for public drunkenness, the processing routine of street-police-court-jail-street, interspersed with stays in mental hospitals, hospitals, welfare homes, missions, and court-required work-therapy programs, has been known as "the revolving door." The rehabilitation process following the implementation of the Uniform Act is now also seen to be a revolving door. Indeed, it is seen as a "padded revolving door" by Fagan and Mauss (1978).

The concept of the revolving door is in wide currency, for example, with Pittman and Gordon (1958), Wiseman (1970), Nimmer (1972), Bahr (1973), Gallant et al. (1973), and Blumberg, Shipley, and Shandler (1973) as cited by Fagan and Mauss (1978). Fagan and Mauss' (1978) data from Seattle before and after the implementation of the Uniform Act show that the likelihood of recidivism in public-drunkenness cases quadrupled with the implementation of the Uniform Act in 1975. In 1973, 65 percent of Skid Row arrestees in Seattle were picked up only one time, and 115 were arrested five times or more. In 1975, with the Uniform Act in force, 27 percent were one timers and 46 percent were five-time or more repeaters (Fagan and Mauss 1978). Fagan and Mauss suggest that:

> The old revolving-door process has become much softer and more pleasant with the detox centers than it was with the drunk tanks and jail sentences. There is nothing to stop the chronic Skid Road inebriate from getting himself admitted to the detox center, with its comfortable accommodations and friendly staff, two or three times in a given week. . . . In other words, one can go on indefinitely interspersing a few days of drunkenness with a few days of good meals, clean beds, and drying out at the detox center, and all this at public expense if one is indigent. Far from intervening in the revolving-door cycle, the arrangements under the new Uniform Act may simply be facilitating the perpetuation of a Skid Road life-style for most of the targeted clients. [1978, p. 32]

Opposition

If by 1977 only twenty states had adopted the Uniform Act after its 1972 drafting, then the existence of opposition may be inferred. Interestingly, perhaps because new programs for dealing with public inebriates are promoted as rehabilitative, opposition is generated. Rehabilitation of the long-time Skid Row man is neither simple nor likely to be permanent. Costs of public-inebriate programs are seen as high and promising to grow. For this reason, in Philadelphia, after a court ruling that habitual intoxication was an illness rather than a criminal offense, Shandler (1972) identified the city administration as the bottleneck in changing jurisdiction over the habitual intoxicant away from the police and courts. Manos (1975) identifies similar roots of opposition to the Bowery project and probably other programs as well.

Opposition has also been voiced on other grounds. For example, the staffs of the Seattle missions went on record as opposed to free shelter three years before that city's detox center opened. Mission personnel were concerned that a facility that is too attractive encourages the immigration of persons. Also, programs that do not expect repayment stifle a man's motivation to be self-sustaining (Ruppert 1972b).

The Funding Process: Bureaucracy

If objections to implementation of social-service plans for Skid Row men have been based on resistance to spending money and on moral conviction about supporting persons who do not work, it has been so primarily at the city level. Much of the financing of services to Skid Row men has been federal. The growth of services to Skid Row may be better understood in view of the funding process of the bureaucratic entities involved. City-administration opposition to a national shift in policy may be softened when outside funding is forthcoming and new programs can be fit into existing agencies without further commitment of city funds, at least no more than absolutely necessary. For example, the Model Cities Program was at first administratively part of HUD. It was soon placed under the direct supervision of mayors. Model Cities demonstration projects were often initiated with the condition that city or other monies would carry on the project after the demonstration period proved the project's worth. Many projects folded after initial funding.

Since funding continuity is somewhat tenuous, social-service agencies, or divisions of them, or projects of social-service agencies are occasionally threatened with impending loss of funding. With some agencies, the threat is yearly. For employees this situation is uncomfortable and often severely damaging to office morale and sense of purpose. Staff turnover is sometimes high. One agency or subagency response to this situation is to branch out, both in function and funding sources. *Grantsmanship* and *empire building* are terms that describe this process. Grantsmanship is the ability to write proposals to funding bodies that will assure the continuing functioning of an office. Empire building is the development of projects that become functional and bureaucratic entities in themselves but still as divisions of an office. These divisions sometimes become independent, growing entities in themselves and are called "spin-off" projects. Grant monies distributed by branches of the federal and state governments and by private foundations are provided to groups and projects that promise to implement certain goals of the funding bodies. Tying one's own capabilities, existing staff, and office space to these goals and associated money helps in the maintenance of an organized staff, or any staff. An accusation, more or less applicable to various social-service agencies, is that efforts expended for office survival run ahead of efforts expended in service to clients.

With many programs, grantsmanship is barely necessary. State and local governments are sometimes simply presented by the federal government with opportunities for funding if they will develop particular programs. Sometimes funding is contingent on a local agreement to maintain the program or contribute a certain percentage of the program's costs. The contribution percentage is often made in kind—that is, with some sort of service the city is already set up to give, such as accounting, police, fire, water, and legal services. These often cost the city no additional payments.

Summary

Through the process described in the previous sections, Skid Row men have been the target population for numerous new service programs. However, with all the new social services available to Skid Row residents, it cannot be said that the social-service component of the plans to abolish Skid Row has been as successful as the demolition component. Basically, what has happened is that the former degrading aspects of Skid Row have been replaced by more-humane services. The missions have shrunk in number, and the drunk tank is a thing of the past in many places. From the analysis of Fagan and Mauss (1978), it appears (at least in Seattle) that the Skid Row drinker (only part of the Skid Row population) has been subsidized in his life-style. It is not clear that detoxification and long-term-rehabilitation facilities are any more successful in rehabilitation than the missions and the police were in the past. According to an impact study of the Uniform Act (CTSAA 1976), cited by Fagan and Mauss (1978), very few of even the most incapacitated accept referral from detox. Few who do accept referral actually report, and few who do report ever complete the treatment.

Skid Row Revival?

Serious debate exists over whether Skid Row is declining permanently even in the physical sense, much less in the social-behavioral sense. Wiseman

(1970) discounts the disappearance of Skid Row, arguing that no U.S. city has yet been successful in eradicating the area of the homeless man with its characteristic institutions. More evidence against Skid Row's disappearance is found in a 1972 New York City Budget Bureau report noting growth of that city's single-room-occupancy population. The report urged that the city council rescind a new housing code that would have eliminated single-room-occupancy buildings by 1977 (*The New York Times* 1972). A major point in the debate over Skid Row elimination is that its population and size fluctuates inversely with the strength of the economy. The 1960s were a boom time unequaled previously. As inflation cuts real earnings, and as growth of the economy slows, can we expect a revival of Skid Row?

In earlier times when the economy was less controlled, rapid fluctuations on Skid Row were observed. Anderson (1923, p. 259) reports, for example, that the Jewish Social Service Bureau's homeless-men department gave 1,333 men personal and material aid in 1921. During 1922, the number of men aided fell to less than half this number due largely to an improved industrial situation. Similarly, the years 1908 and 1914 were high-unemployment years. For example, the Chicago Municipal Lodging House provided 23,642 lodgings in 1907 and 105,564 in 1908, 78,392 in 1913, and 452,361 in 1914. In 1918 and 1919, this house closed for lack of applicants (Anderson 1923, pp. 260–261).

In more-recent times, rapid growth of the Skid Row population has also been observed. While the more-virile members of the Skid Row population—for instance, local workingmen and transients who are primarily laborers—are greatly diminished in numbers, other classes of the Skid Row population may well experience dramatic growth. Besser (1975, p. 51) writes of a "Skid Row explosion" in which especially young men are flooding rescue misisons coast to coast. Young unmarried men without job prospects and young family men deserting so their families become eligible for Aid to Families with Dependent Children are joining growing numbers of elderly pensioners who have inadequate income to live anywhere but on Skid Row. Besser also identifies other sources of recent increases in the Skid Row population. For example, Social Security benefits have not kept pace with inflation, pressuring more people to the missions. Newcomers to Skid Row also include young and middle-aged men who have spent much of their lives in institutions, only to be released with budgetary cutbacks and reclassification of clients. Besser (1975) further notes an increase on Skid Row in the number of physically ill persons whose resources have been exhausted. Also, much more noticeably than in the past, whole families are participating in Skid Row means of survival.

As mentioned before, Besser identifies still another dimension of movement to Skid Row—youth. Mission superintendents in Chicago and Milwaukee reported to Besser that 10 to 20 percent of the men passing through their institutions are in the eighteen-to-twenty-year-old age range, a group that has been almost entirely absent from the Skid Row scene since the worst days of the Depression. Most of these youths are semiskilled or unskilled. Others are "a strange fallout from the countercultural 1960s: intelligent, from fairly affluent backgrounds, and highly alienated . . . filled with the deadening apathy which took the old-timers years to develop" (Besser 1975, p. 52).

The influx of youths into Skid Row was also identified in *Newsweek* (1974, p. 68) as a continuation of the attitudes, behavior patterns, and lack of health manifest by older Skid Row men. The article quoted a Los Angeles mission director who observed that during the Depression, skilled workers populated Skid Row. During the war, servicemen were the most observable component of Skid Row. At present, the influx of young people is striking. According to the article, the young and the old habitués maintain an easy truce. In 1981, a Los Angeles writer (Secter 1981, p. 1) referred to Skid Row as a growing phenomenon with an unusually large proportion of clean-cut men in their twenties and thirties.

Bahr's (1967) data (correspondence with city officials) indicate that the decline of the traditional Skid Row was often not seen as the equivalent of the disappearance of the homeless population. Bahr (1974, p. 51) concludes, "In general, however, there is little evidence that the absolute number of homeless men is declining." However, he points to a mechanism whereby this number might be reduced:

> With the dispersion of Skid Row men and the transformation of the Skid Row area to other patterns of land use, homeless men will no longer have to bear the stigma of Skid Row residence. The absence of this stigma should facilitate their rehabilitation. [Bahr 1974, p. 51]

Lee (1978a) finds that Skid Row census-tract population-composition characteristics are not fluctuating greatly but show a rise in the proportion of women and an increase in status. These changes could be due to new apartments' not serving low-income men.

Seattle's Skid Road as a Case Study

The specific setting of this book's empirical investigation is Seattle's Skid Road area and other possibly emergent Skid Rows in Seattle and in other Washington coastal cities. Seattle's Skid Road has fared very much as other Skid Row areas around the country. Its history is somewhat peculiar and so is its Skid Road area. A logging and port city built on steep hills with a founding date of 1852, Seattle carried frontier roughness well into the twentieth century. As civility first drew the deadline in Seattle, north of which no bawdyhouse-saloon behavior would be tolerated, it more or less steadily cordoned and contained prostitution, public drunkenness, and fights to "Skid Road: the place of dead dreams" (Morgan 1960, p. 7). Skid Road declined of natural causes much as Skid Rows of other cities up through the 1960s. The 1960s were high times for Seattle, with a profitable world's fair in 1962 and direct Boeing employment in the Seattle metropolitan area at over 100,000 (Morgan 1960).

The management of Skid Road has been similar to management of Skid Rows elsewhere. In the three-year period including 1968, 1969, and 1970, 52.5 percent of all of the 67,484 arrests in the city of Seattle involved intoxication. Of these, only 11.4 percent involved driving under the influence of alcohol. Of the remaining 31,408 drunkenness arrests in the three-year period, 2,784 men and 74 women were arrested in the census tract that includes the CBD of Seattle. Second only to the CBD in the drunk-arrest rate is the Skid Road–area census tract with 1,638 men and 91 women arrested. However, of those arrested in the CBD, 871 resided in the Skid Road census tract. However, census-tract figures do not relate the total contribution of Skid Row men to drunk-arrest statistics. Five hundred people arrested in the CBD had no known address, which is typical of many Skid Row men. Also, the census tracts adjacent to Skid Road contributed disproportionately to the drunk-arrest count as did census tracts some distance away but heavily populated by persons whose circumstances are in some ways not different from men residing in the traditional Skid Road area (Schmid and Schmid 1972).

In Seattle, business interests have been seen as pitted against the Skid Road residential community. Cleaning up the streets is less the problem than justifying dislocating Skid Road people. In Seattle, as in many cities, land values in downtown areas have risen, and business development and renovation are progressing rapidly. Conflict was explicit in the invasion of Skid Road. A prime figure in the restoration of the historic Skid Road area of Seattle made the statement that in the late 1960s a choice was made between having a social conscience and commercial development. The developer indicated that free enterprise was the choice made (Ruppert 1972a).

From January 1970 to January 1972, forty hotels and buildings chiefly in the Seattle Skid Road and adjacent areas were demolished, thus eliminating 2,732 housing units. Few Skid Road hotels could afford to improve to meet strict city standards (Ruppert 1972a). A downtown stadium in Seattle, completed in 1975, has further depressed the residential nature of the Skid Road area. In 1973, the last mission in Seattle that would give a bed to a man, drunk or sober, closed its doors for the last time after the ancient, dark building that housed it was sold and closed for renovation. Now, at the northwest corner of the intersection of First Avenue and Washington Street is a charming old building. Other missions still take in the sober.

While recent Skid Row–area closings seem precipitous, a set of expert views identifies them as merely the culmination of a trend extending back twenty years or so. Three long-termed wine distributors in Seattle described the present Skid Road as barely identifiable as such when compared to the recent past.

Seattle has not, however, demolished buildings to the extent other cities may have. Historical interest in the Skid Road area has been keen. In telling of the move toward preservation rather than demolition, the mayor of Seattle from 1968 to 1978 related that he would not grant permits to use property as a parking lot in the interim period between demolition and new construction. He said the city would also waive modern building-code requirements and "cut red tape at City Hall" to encourage fixing up a building (Brashear 1978, p. 6A). These tactics were described by the former mayor as necessary because Washington prevents government financial assistance for private development. In addition to historical and tourist value, investors have financial interest. According to the former mayor, historical buildings are an excellent tax write-off (Brashear 1978, p. 6A).

Seattle may be unusual in its affection for Skid Road. Not only the buildings are historical, but the Skid Road men are, too. The former mayor reported delighting in welcoming visitors to the city with an invitation to visit Skid Road. "I was the only mayor in America who could do that," he mused (Brashear 1978, p. 6A). The former mayor described Pioneer Square as still serving Seattle's Skid Row people, pointing out that the street people have access to a city-operated shelter facility near Pioneer Square as well as a medical-treatment facility. The difference nowadays, he said, is that Skid Road is not the exclusive domain of Skid Row people. They share the area with visitors and others.

In other respects, Seattle's Skid Road as a case study may be more typical. An example of the grantsmanship that has served Skid Row is the Skid Road Community Council (SRCC). This organization originated as part of the war on poverty in the 1960s. First funded by Model Cities, this group has received support from several branches of government, including a $540,500 grant from the National Institute of Mental Health for an alcoholic-treatment program, a $90,000 grant to lease and renovate an old hotel to provide lodging and services for Skid Road residents, and a state grant to provide various other services to area residents. The staff managed these projects and counseled and distributed meal and lodging tickets to those who came to their office in need, and it functioned as a referral agency. Part of the renovated hotel is a coffee bar with magazines, billiards, chairs, and couches. It provides a place for one to go to pass time out of the weather. At one time, this place was reputedly a hangout for drug addicts. Competition

and tension existed between the SRCC and the missions. The SRCC personnel pointed out the need for services that residents have regardless of religious persuasion. The council no longer exists, but the hotel project initiated by it is now the shelter facility referred to by the former mayor.

Nevertheless, in spite of the major's professed tolerance for Skid Road
men, and despite the fact that the city operates a shelter facility, Seattle's
Skid Road population has felt the same pressures as Skid Row populations
elsewhere. For example, hotels close every year; missions are evicted for
fashionable renovation; cheap cafes go out of business; and taverns
upgrade and are no longer hospitable to Skid Road clientele. Apparently, in
the 1960s and even more in the 1970s the facilities and services in Seattle
serving Skid Road have been reduced to a greater extent than natural
decrease in the Skid Road population would have warranted. This pressure
makes Seattle at least a somewhat representative case study of the problem
of relocation of a subculture whose former natural habitat has been invaded
by more-powerful groups.

Conclusion

Skid Row areas across the country have been diminished considerably
through urban-renewal demolition and private renovation. This action has
followed a decrease in the economic function of Skid Row as a homing area
for transient labor. Social services created for Skid Row men during and
after the physical diminution of Skid Row professed rehabilitation as their
goal. Rehabilitation has not occurred on a large scale, and recruitment to
the Skid Row life-style continues. Thus, these agencies do not seem to be
"running the bums out of town" after all, but town is not what it used to
be. Skid row may never go away, but the more feeble may be better cared
for in their days of greatest inability, possibly whether they want to be or
not. If Skid Row means disease, alcoholism, and malnutrition—and it
does—it may be diminished by the present social-service strategy. If Skid
Row is life on the bum—and it is—it will not be diminished but will rather
be made easier for those people willing to institutionalize themselves. Probably most Skid Row men will not colonize detoxification and treatment
facilities other than temporarily. The restrictions are too great and the open
road, or at least the freedom of a bench in the park, is still a part of the subculture. Thus, the question to be addressed in the next chapters is: Where
will all the Skid Rowers go when Skid Row is gone?

2

Where Do the Dogs Bark?

Hark! Hark! The dogs do bark.
The beggars are coming to town.
Some in rags, some in tags,
And some in velvet gowns.

—Nursery rhyme

While there has been a natural decrease in at least one segment of Skid Row due to decreased use of unskilled day labor, more-humane hiring practices, and overall prosperity, it would appear that the sharp decreases in Skid Row characteristics experienced in most U.S. cities in the 1960s and 1970s would have been slower had not intensive, federally funded efforts occurred to physically eliminate Skid Row from the urban mosaic. The question remains: Where did all the old, young, able, and not-so-able Skid Row men go? Since a large proportion of Skid Row institutions have disappeared, and since the area is largely diminished as a distinctive area, what has happened to the people and the behaviors that characterized the area as it existed in the past? Have they relocated? Since urban-renewal action cleaned up most Skid Row areas in the United States, where does the individual without affiliation go? When the open asylum of Skid Row is sharply reduced in ability to accommodate, where do the regulars and the recruits go? What is the alternative to the skids? Varying degrees of insight in the formation of probable answers may be gleaned from the field of human ecology and from theories of urban development and intraurban migration, as well as from a few other sources.

The Theoretical Vista

Two theoretical approaches appear to offer insight and, more or less directly, imply specific answers to the question at hand. Broadly, the two approaches are the ecological-spatial theories and the cultural-values theories. In this chapter, focusing first on ecological theories then cultural theories, the discussion will move from more-abstract and -general to specific formulations. After explication of each theory, or the parts of it most

27

relevant to the question at hand, apparent implied predictions for Skid Row location after displacement are discussed. These implied predictions are summarized at the end of the chapter.

Ecological-Spatial Theories

Two important, overlapping sets of conceptualizations representing a historic divergence in the field of human ecology are the works of Quinn (1950) and Hawley (1950). Hawley's work has essentially eclipsed Quinn's. Hawley applies the wholistic world view of the ecologist to "the human aggregate"—that is, he focuses on concepts from the field of ecology and their application to the habitat of people, population growth and characteristics, organization of people along various lines for various reasons, and the change and development of communities. Hawley applies concepts and theories of ecology to human-energy transformations and accumulations. Quinn's text is a summary and organization of the findings and generalizations of the human-ecology studies of sociologists at the University of Chicago. The divergence, not created by the two 1950 tomes, is identified by Dunlap and Catton (1978, p. 4) as, on one side, a "realistic approach to influences of a physical world upon human society" and, on the other side, "advancing reliance (for explanation) in social exchange." It is well beyond the scope of this study to review the works of Hawley and Quinn in their entirety. Thus, our focus is limited to aspects of their texts that can be more or less directly applied to the question of Skid Row location.

Quinn's Areal Concepts and Hypotheses. Quinn provides a solid base of concepts related to areal structure that are of use in theoretically examining the question of Skid Row location. *Zone* is defined in various ways, among them being (1) a natural area (definition following), (2) a formal spatial area with no implication of homogeneity or functional organization, and (3) a designation used in governmental control of utilization patterns. The term *natural area* is defined by Quinn as:

> [A]ny particular extent of the earth's surface that has come to be distinctive through the unplanned operation of ecological or social processes. Chief emphasis in this concept historically has centered on the fact that such areas depend more on the nondeliberate, nonplanned operation of interactional processes than on deliberate design and planned areal control. [1950, pp. 266–267]

Dominance means greater influence or control by one unit over others or that one unit has an integrative function that regulates the activities of others. *Distance* of three types is distinguished by Quinn: linear, ecological, and social. Linear distance is simple separation. Ecological distance is similar but its measurement depends on the cost of moving people and materials through space. Social distance involves perceived status difference and, usually, affective distance. Three kinds of *position* correspond to the three types of distance. Geometric position is a purely spatial concept. Two types of ecological position may be distinguished: ecological-spatial position, involving both ecological distance from a reference base and direction from this base along available transportation routes; and ecological-functional position, location of a unit within a dominance-subordination relation within a functional network. Spatial position is central in area analysis. The concept of *gradient* refers to the rate of increase or decrease of a variable across a given linear distance. *Functional chain* is a concept used primarily in biological ecology, refering to links between types of organisms in satisfying, collectively, each of their various biological needs. The position occupied by any species within such a chain is a *niche*. Position of any unit in a functional chain is a niche. According to Quinn, in human ecology the concepts functional chain and niche have been useful in studying the numbers of functional units of a given type needed within any niche in a stable, efficient economy.

Quinn has formulated four hypotheses dealing with areal structure. The first and most general is the hypothesis of *minimum costs:*

> Ecological units tend to distribute themselves throughout an area so that the total costs of gaining maximum satisfaction in adjusting population to environment (including other men) are reduced to the minimum. Or, stated another way, ecological units tend to distribute themselves throughout an area so that with costs constant, the total net satisfactions that result from the adjustments of the population to environment (including other men) are raised to the maximum. [1950, p. 282]

In connection with this hypothesis, and qualifying it, Quinn discusses the nonmaterial costs and competitive strength of different units, and he acknowledges that the historic inertia of custom or dead laws sometimes operates to prevent the utilization of a location by the ecological unit that could occupy it most efficiently.

Second, a corollary of the hypothesis of minimum costs is the hypothesis of *minimum ecological distance,* which refers to the costs involved in transporting people and materials from place to place:

> If other factors are constant within an area, ecological units tend to distribute themselves throughout it so that the total ecological distance traversed in adjusting to limited environmental factors, including other ecological and social units, is reduced to the minimum. (1950, pp. 285-286]

Quinn states that this hypothesis has particular value in analyzing the spatial structure of functionally organized areas and that it helps explain why specialized ecological units tend to assume typical spatial patterns, especially where local environmental differences do not afford an adequate explanation.

Third, the hypothesis of *median location* is a special application of the minimum-distance hypothesis, stating that the minimum costs of transportation for a given unit will be achieved when it locates at the median. It is stated by Quinn as follows:

> Within a free competitive system, social and aesthetic factors being equal, a mobil ecological unit tends to occupy a median location with respect to (1) the environmental resources it utilizes, (2) the other units on which it depends, and (3) the other units that it serves. [1950, p. 286]

The adjustment between people and resources includes people's moving about an area to collect the resources they use, resources' being transported to people, or both. Whatever units move across ecological distances, these units must be counted in determining the median. Quinn observes that the hypothesis of median location aids in explaining the spatial distribution of nonprofit service centers, retail stores, industries, cities, and homes. Hopefully, it will also aid in predicting Skid Row location.

Fourth, when different types of ecological units compete with one another for a given location—the same median location, for example—Quinn predicts the outcome with what he terms the hypothesis of *intensiveness of utilization:*

> That ecological unit tends to occupy the common median which can utilize it most intensively. [1950, p. 288]

Intensiveness of utilization may depend on either the direct utilization of resources or the degree of increased ecological distance that would result if one or the other competitor moved. The one tends to occupy a space whose removal would result in the greatest increase of ecological distance. This increase could be determined by the number of customers, for example, that would have to travel farther to get to a particular establishment.

Quinn points out that certain assumptions are present in stating these hypotheses. One assumption is that organisms utilize resources of the physical environment, including other organisms, to satisfy their needs and that they attempt to escape recognized dangers and discomforts. Another assumption is that humans tend to follow the line of least resistance in obtaining resources and avoiding dangers and in maintaining desired contacts with other people. This does not necessarily imply wise action. Partial knowledge is usually the basis for action. Unconscious neurotic behavior, as well as cultural biases, may also influence behavior. A third assumption Quinn identifies is that specific wants and the recognition of resources, dangers, and barriers depend on culture and are not understandable apart from it. Social needs as well as biological needs influence behavior. However, resources for the satisfaction of wants are limited, and the increasing or decreasing of limited factors of the environment explains areal structure and change. Traditional patterns of settlement, social ties, and prejudices also make a precise application of these hypotheses to real ecological units in real areas difficult. Past accumulations of nonmobile, or nearly so, institutions in an area enter the variable of history into the phenomena these hypotheses seek to explain. Nevertheless, with pertinent information—for example, characteristics and situations of Skid Row—these hypotheses can be applied to the question of Skid Row location following dispersal.

The application of Quinn's hypotheses to Skid Row location must be in terms of the wants and circumstances of Skid Row men, and they vary as do those of any other social category. However, if the wants of an ideal-type Skid Row man were to be identified, they would include, perhaps in order, the availability of cheap or free places to eat and sleep; recreational opportunities at little or no cost, if only a place to stand, sit, or lie to watch the passing scene; the opportunity to earn money (if not on pension or welfare); and available liquor and the freedom to drink without harassment. The resources for satisfying these wants include abandoned buildings and cars; railroad cars; cheap rooming houses and hotels; food stores; commercial-food-establishment garbage cans; cheap restaurants; missions and mission-like institutions; liquor stores and cheap, more-or-less-hospitable taverns; casual-labor employment agencies; plasma-collection centers; and parks, public squares, and other loitering places where one is not obviously eyed with malice or disgust.

Minimizing costs, especially local-transportation costs, implies, for Skid Row men, living close to the services. Transportation for Skid Row men in the city is virtually all on foot, and transportation routes are sidewalks and alleys. The primary cost of transportation is simple physical effort. There is also a moving-traffic danger to pedestrians, especially when drunk, though except for arterial traffic this is probably largely uncalculated. If hand carrying is one's only method of transporting groceries and other goods, one will probably choose one's location of residence and activities carefully. Another usually insignificant matter for most people in this country today—an available restroom—is no small concern for Skid Row men. Readily available drinking water is also sometimes a problem. People in more-typical, affiliated life-styles invariably have water provided for them in institutional activities. Indoor occupations are shielded from the need for drinking water by air conditioning. If our ideal-type Skid Row man does not sit in his hotel lobby all day, he may risk disapproving glares, verbal abuse, or a long walk to get a drink of water. It is much pleasanter to be thirsty near places where these problems do not happen—namely, on Skid Row where one is not exceptional.

The median-location hypothesis also predicts that Skid Row would be relatively compact if choices of Skid Row men for the median spot were to prevail. Given the location of services and opportunities peculiar to the Skid Row life-style, this location has been and, according to Quinn's theory, should continue to be in the area immediately surrounding the CBD, where property values are high and property improvements nil. As noted, however, competition for the traditional Skid Row median-location choice has recently been keen, not among Skid Row men but between Skid Row uses and other interests. The functional niche of the Skid Row man and his competitive strength in intensively utilizing the fringe of the CBD have diminished with changes in the composition of the Skid Row population. The question may be posed whether the open-asylum-maintenance function of Skid Row, along with remnants of the hobo/tramp/bum subculture, can ever again utilize an area intensively enough, competitively enough, to claim it as their own, or to gain for an area a reputation like Skid Row has had. Because of a decreasing intensity of utilization of land by the Skid Row subculture and a decreasing availability of the resources Skid Row men weakly compete for, a possibility suggested by Quinn's intensity-of-utilization hypothesis is that no distinct area exists that the Skid Row life-style will most intensively use. Another hypothesis, implied by all of Quinn's hypotheses, coupled with the declining functional importance of Skid Row, is that Skid Row men will continue making choices to minimize their costs and that those choices will continue to locate them in the Skid Row area. However, such choices will mean that they will incur greater ecological, or logistical, costs—that is, they will be spread out more.

A rationale exists for yet another specific hypothesis. Since the physical plant of Skid Row has been in large part destroyed for Skid Row use, the median location of Skid Row men's services may not be as clear or as apparent a choice as it once was. Choice of location may focus around more than one median. This would result in a dividing of Skid Row into clusters. This may be a particularly relevant hypothesis in light of the now orientation identified by Wiseman (1970) and Orwell (1933). Maximum satisfaction for the Skid Row man is often a matter of finding something interesting to do and finding the least expensive food on a daily or even hourly basis.

These hypotheses, drawn from knowledge of the Skid Row subculture and Quinn's human-ecology hypotheses, are summarized, along with several hypotheses yet to be discussed, at the end of the chapter.

Hawley on Natural Area and Symbiosis. The section of Hawley's (1950) book that is most directly relevant to Skid Row is perhaps his discussion of natural areas. Hawley (1950, pp. 80–81) defines the geographical concept of the natural area as an area physically delimited, for example, by rivers, coastlines, mountains, and so on. In the social-science use of the term, Hawley notes a transition toward including physically distinct territorial units, even when such units are created or conditioned by human activities. The natural area has come to mean an area of a uniform physical type bounded, for example, by an elongated building, railroad tracks, arterial thoroughfares, or other similar features. Hawley also discusses the anthropological term *cultural area* and the correlation of natural areas and cultural areas. In considering the issue of natural-area characteristics as *causing* behavior, Hawley discounts the early geographical determinism of Ratzel (1897; 1898) and others. However, he traces the transition of the concept of region among geographers from the strictly physiogeographic to an area within which the combination of environmental and demographic factors has created a homogeneity of economic and social structure. The natural area in sociological use, according to Hawley (1950, pp. 89–90), is one of "more-or-less-uniform composition, particularly in regard to type, congestion, and degree of deterioration of buildings: sometimes such factors as location, altitude, and street pattern are also included." A natural area usually "comprises a particular kind of population with respect to social heritage, occupation, interests, or other distinguishing cultural possessions." While Hawley states that habitat factors are certainly not the sole determinants of behavior, based on a large number of studies, specifically those of McKensie (1921–1922), Thrasher (1927), Wirth (1928), Zorbaugh (1929), Shaw (1929), Faris and Dunham (1939), Hoyt (1939), and Bowers (1939), he does allow that a correlation exists between the physical characteristics of natural areas in the city and certain behavior patterns (1950, p. 90). Perhaps Skid Row is such an area, a role setting. As pilots need airports and doctors need clinics and hospitals, so also may Skid Row men need Skid Row. This implies rather directly that the destruction of the physical area of Skid Row could mean the end of characteristic Skid Row behavior in a more-direct manner than Bahr (1974) suggests—namely, by removing the stigma of Skid Row and thereby allowing for rehabilitation.

Hawley's discussion of symbiosis, a mutual dependence between unlike organisms, has direct bearing on Skid Row as well. Sometimes the relationship between the Skid Row men and the missions has been termed symbiotic (Bibby and Mauss 1974). It has also been identified as either of two subforms of symbiosis: parasitism and helotism (helotism in biology is the enslavement of one species by another). The obvious prediction from this group of observations is that where there are missions there will be Skid Row men and vice versa. Missions should count heavily in determining the desirable median location for Skid Row dwellings and activities.

Urban-Development Models. Three widely cited models of city development offer some predictions for the location of our displaced population of interest. The best known is probably Burgess's (1929) *concentric-zone* theory. Briefly, the model is that as a city grows it expands in rings of growth around the CBD. Each ring continues to grow outward. Burgess identified five zones: (1) the CBD; (2) the zone in transition, encroached upon by the growing or shifting CBD and containing some of the oldest buildings in the city, the area where land values are high and rents are low, the area of homeless men; (3) the zone of independent workingmen's homes that encircles the zone in transition; (4) the zone of better residences; and (5) the commuter zone including the so-called bedroom-community suburbs. Burgess's model simply predicts that Skid Row will remain in the transition zone, perhaps shifting slightly away from the CBD or moving around it.

A second prominent model of the growth and spatial structuring of U.S. cites is Hoyt's (1939) *sector* theory. As explained by Nelson (1971, p. 79), Hoyt analyzed the distribution of residential neighborhoods defined by rent levels, and found that similar rent neighborhoods clustered along radii. Hoyt argued that if a sector of the city first develops as a high-, medium-, or low-rental residential area, it will tend to retain that character for long distances as the sector extends outward through the process of the city's growth. Sectors have their own cycle of "filtering"—that is, the process of the housing demand of lower-income groups met by their moving into housing vacated by a higher-income group. According to Smith (1971, p. 170), citing Ratcliff (1949, p. 321), filtering was the dynamic element in Hoyt's sector theory. Hoyt also noted that the area occupied by the highest income families tends to be on high ground; on a lake, river, or ocean shore; or along the fastest existing transportation route and close to country clubs or parks on the periphery. Lowest income families tended to live in sectors farthest from the high-rent areas and alongside railroad, industrial, or commercial areas. Hoyt found that occupants of houses in the low-rent categories tend to move out in bands from the center of the city, moving into houses left behind by higher-income groups. Nelson (1971, p. 79) writes, "It is felt by some that because Hoyt's model takes into account both distance and direction from the center of the city, it is an improvement on the earlier Burgess effort." If a prediction of skid row location following dispersal can be inferred from Hoyt's model and findings, it is that Skid Row will move farther from the CBD, probably in the sector or corridor it occupies, or that it will move into a toehold position in a new sector whose inhabitants are leaving.

The third model, that of Harris and Ullman (1945), argues that the land-use pattern of a city does not grow from a single center but from nuclei of functional units in various parts of the city. The nuclei may be centers in existence since the city's early growth, such as communities engulfed by the city, or they can develop during the growth of the city, such as a factory area. According to Nelson (1971), four factors are seen by Harris and Ullman to account for the rise of separate nuclei and differentiated districts. First, certain activities require specialized facilities—for example, a port requires a harbor. Second, certain similar activities are grouped together because they profit from linkages—for example, wholesale activities may cluster together to facilitate comparison shopping. Third, certain dissimilar activities are detrimental to each other—for example, bulk storage is not compatible with retail sales. Fourth, certain enterprises are unable to afford the high rents of desirable locations—for example, tattoo parlors are seldom located in CBD skyscrapers. Possible Skid Row locations following dispersal suggested by this model are areas away from the CBD but adjacent to nuclei of the older, engulfed communities that could support Skid Row functions.

Nelson (1971, p. 80) acknowledges that with large- and medium-sized cities, elements of each of these three models can be recognized, and he writes that "there has been extensive statistical testing of these models in recent years with no conclusive results. [However,] they remain as valuable conceptual tools for analyzing the modern city." The Seattle research reported in this work may help determine how valuable the concepts are.

Intracity-Migration Theories. Stouffer's (1940) theory relating mobility and distance identifies three factors influencing intraurban migration. The volume of migration from one urban subarea to another depends inversely on the distance, directly on the number of opportunities at that distance, and inversely on the number of opportunities at lesser distances. Various areas offer certain opportunities to a displaced Skid Row population. The opportunities may include low-cost lodging, short-term-employment opportunities, free food, places to comfortably pass the time, and so on. Stouffer's theory implies that Skid Row men will follow or be attracted to Skid Row institutions and opportunities. If institutions are primary, then in order for a new Skid Row area to develop, institutions must break ground in a new area in a sort of blockbusting manner. This could simply involve a change in the practice of making Skid Row patrons unwelcome, or it could mean the actual relocation of institutions such as missions or casual-labor offices. These establishments usually maintain addresses in buildings in Burgess's second zone—that adjacent to the CBD. Thus, a prediction implied by Stouffer's theory is that a displaced Skid Row area will relocate around institutions that will probably remain in the area adjacent to the CBD.

In the study of intraurban migration, the decision-making process has been identified by Brown and Moore (1971) and Lee (1978a) as a topic of recent emphasis in the understanding of such migration. Basically, the process involves stress factors that prompt members of a household to decide to move. The potential movers define aspirations for a new dwelling, search information sources for dwelling vacancies, examine vacancies, and decide to change residences. A decision to remain is also possible. *Search space* reflects distinct social, economic, and spatial characteristics. One observation made by Brown and Moore (1971) relevant to Skid Row location is that locations of vacancies discovered through interpersonal communications are limited by the configuration of the intending migrant's acquaintance circle and by the awareness spaces of the acquaintances contained within that circle. Because Bahr (1973) characterizes the Skid Row population as geographically restricted, and because hotels catering to Skid Row men do not advertise, we might assume that Skid Row men move to places they learn of through word of mouth, or even more limiting, by walking. This line of reasoning predicts short-distance moves—that is, Skid Row will remain close to its present area.

Regarding migration of a group to a new area, Hawley (1950) writes that an information flow to migrating groups precedes their influx into a new area and that pioneers precede mass movements. This is a prediction relevant to our focus on Seattle in that Schmid and Schmid (1972), in reporting drunk-arrest locations and home addresses of those arrested for drunkenness in Seattle, note that in two outlying areas in Seattle—Ballard and Fremont—several men with Skid Road addresses were picked up, indicating that the formation of satellite Skid Row areas is a plausible hypothesis.

Smith (1971) describes the process of invasion and the mechanism through which that process occurs. Smith writes that the filtering down of good residences to progressively lower-status occupants does not occur in the lowest income group. He cites Rodwin's (1950) point that the real estate market is a notorious and often cited example of market imperfections. The concept of filtering is passive, whereas the actual process of movement of lower-income persons can be seen as an active process, as Rose (1971, p. 320) shows in identifying circumstances in which racial invasion triggers a drop in prices. Rose writes that with the movement of the ghetto the unwillingness of whites to compete with nonwhites for housing in a common housing market causes rising vacancy rates. Vacancy rates rise faster than the rate of nonwhite demand, which leads to a reduction in property values.

This discussion implies that a mechanism exists whereby Skid Row could regroup rather than disappear. The stigma of Skid Row could be an asset in acquiring new quarters. This could be true in Seattle in spite of the somewhat more-favorable status Skid Road men have there as opposed to Skid Row men elsewhere. Evidence indicates that some Seattle merchants, especially tavern operators, have negative attitudes toward some Skid Road men, attitudes similar to those observed near the Bowery and cited in chapter 1.

A view of the phenomenon of intracity migration in historical perspective is given by Roebuck and by analogy is applicable to Skid Row:

The demolition of dilapidated buildings to make room for parking lots, convention centers, and office buildings removes the symptoms of urban blight from the specific areas treated, but it does not cure the disease any more than the clearing of slums for the building of railways and new streets ended the slums in the nineteenth century. Indeed, such cures tend merely to spread the blight and to create new slums outside the cleared areas, for the poor do not vanish with their old homes. They simply move to the next-cheapest and hence least desirable areas in town, creating new slums in areas that before were only dilapidated. [1974, p. 204]

This quotation suggests that Skid Row men, like other poor people, will move to the cheapest places available. This raises a possibility other than the obvious one that another area adjacent to the CBD, which would probably be among the next cheapest in the city, would accommodate the displaced Skid Row. The least expensive housing may sometimes be found, not in the city at all but in smaller population centers of the hinterland. This hypothesis appears viable for another reason: Urban renewal has not affected the aged buildings of most small cities and towns.

Other Theories of Urban Structure. Several other theories of urban structure, focusing on particular factors in the determination of selected variables, offer limited predictions for Skid Row location. Some of these theories also appear to be of very limited relevance, but each has some implication in relation to the problem at hand.

Chapin (1971) identifies a number of economic models of spatial structure and focuses on Wingo's (1961) work as a most systematic and rigorous example. Wingo develops the concept of *transportation demand* that focuses on the spatial relationship between home and work. The demand for movement is the number of trips required to support the production process, and supply is expressed in terms of the capacity of a movement system. In applying the economic concepts of supply and demand to transportation, while focusing on the location of workers' residence, Wingo's central problem is to achieve an equilibrium in the distribution of households of particular rent-paying abilities in relation to sites with a particular structure of rents. To do this, Wingo substitutes transportation for space costs. While this type of theory, developed in relation to the labor force, could be applied to Skid Row analogues of the transportation system, the analogy seems stretched at best.

Cooley's (1894) theory of transportation deals with the relation of all social institutions to the need for transportation. Directly relevant to this study is his chapter on transportation and rent. He points out that an effect of the improvement of urban transportation is to spread people out, thus reducing rent per unit of area. Cooley states the geometrical relationship as follows:

Insofar as rents depend directly upon facility of access to a given center
(whether facility be measured in time or in cost), they vary near the center
inversely as the square of the efficiency of transportation (that is, inversely
as the square of speed, directly as the square of cost). The area of the rent-
yielding circle, on the other hand, varies directly as the square of the efficiency of transportation. [1894, p. 128]

Cooley's examples from the 1800s involve the change from 6 to 12 miles per
hour, and he discusses the time one can afford in moving from point A to
point B. Since speed of transportation in this era of primarily automobile
transportation is relatively constant, the variable that may affect rent more
than time cost is the dollar cost of transportation. Up to 1972, gasoline in
the United States was uniformly around $.30 per gallon. In 1981, with the
price at $1.30 and above, the awareness of the effect of the price on one's
budget may do more than promote the sale of small cars and the use of
mass-transit systems. It may also have the effect of shrinking the distance
people and enterprises are willing to put between themselves and the places
to which they regularly travel. Hence, rents will go up per unit of area in the
city. Increasing population compounds this pressure on rents.

The prediction for Skid Row and for that matter, all urban enterprises,
is continued pressure on institutions that occupy space. As energy costs rise,
the urban sprawl that followed the proliferation of the automobile as the
principal means of intraurban transportation will become more costly.
Rents, according to Cooley's theory, will rise. The marginal utilization of
land by Skid Row institutions will become more tenuous. All Skid Row
institutions utilize land less intensively than CBD establishments, but those
that are not clearly profitable will be increasingly in jeopardy.

Meier's (1962) communications theory, reviewed by Chapin (1971),
consists of an argument that the use of a communications system as a basis
for building a theory of urban growth is valid; a set of requirements for the
communications process; a proposal to construct a representation of the
city from the information content of communications flows, measuring and
recording information in a double-entry accounting system in much the
same manner as origin and destination traffic studies record traffic flows;
and an argument that with the obtaining of a sample of communication
flows in a metropolitan area, information theory can be used to construct a
set of social accounts that can then become the basis for activity systems.
However, according to Chapin (1971, p. 143), "Meier does not indicate
fully the manner in which the framework would be used by a planner in a
predictive application."

Webber's (1963) interrelated-urban-structure approach, as reviewed by
Chapin (1971), also focuses on human interaction by drawing special attention to interaction systems that extend into larger urban realms as well as to
those that fall within a particular metropolitan area. Webber emphasizes

the importance of viewing the city as a dynamic system in action. He traces this feature of urban dynamics through linkages he terms *dependency ties*— that is, relating individuals, groups, firms, and other entities to one another in "operating systems." What goes on within the spatial confines of an urban place must be interpreted in the framework of all the ties that the community may have with the world at large. While this may be an appropriate framework with which to focus on the urban-renewal actions reducing Skid Row, the relevancy of this theory to Skid Row location following dispersion is not yet apparent.

Guttenberg's (1960) approach to urban structure, as reviewed by Chapin (1971), uses *accessibility* as an organizing concept. The extent of distribution of facilities is positively correlated with ease of transportation. Guttenberg is interested in facilities such as work places and trade centers. The analogy between the city as a whole and Skid Row is a bit stretched, though the fact that ease of transportation for Skid Row men—walking—is relatively constant might imply that Skid Row will not disperse beyond the area it now occupies.

Cultural-Values Theories

The second important perspective bearing on the question of Skid Row location involves cultural values. Two variations can be distinguished in relation to the problem of Skid Row: cultural ecology and social engineering.

Firey's Cultural Ecology. Firey (1946; 1947) argues that cultural values determine urban arrangements, at least in some cases. Firey rejects the inevitability of ecological processes such as invasion and competition. He rejects the deterministic nature of Burgess's and Hoyt's models as a denial that social values or ideals can significantly influence land use. Firey's examples of irregular patterns of residential settlement in Boston provide data supportive of his assertion. Supportive of Firey, Murdie (1971) cites Jones's (1962) rejection of the concentric and sector models in Belfast, Ireland. Belfast is another case where identifiable sectors in the urban pattern are best explained by social values rather than physical factors. According to Smith (1971, p. 172), "Perhaps the most imaginative part of Firey's work is his suggestion of a grand balancing of several objectives from among several cultural groups, within the limited confines of the metropolis." Smith (1971, p. 172) goes on to quote Firey (1947, p. 55):

> There is always a problem of allocating space. In such allocation there must always be a *proportionalization of ends* (emphasis Firey's]. This arises out of the fact that every community has a multiplicity of component ends

and not merely one or a few ends. Hence it becomes necessary to achieve a certain "balance of sacrifices" [quotation marks Firey's] in order that every component end of the community will in some degree be attained. [1971, p. 172]

Firey (1946) discusses ecological symbolism, a sort of neighborhood esprit de corps, as a mechanism for the maintenance of neighborhood composition, especially among wealthy neighborhoods.

The potential importance of Firey's point of view is demonstrated in an article by Alonso (1971), who argues that deterministic models are the basis for the urban-renewal program and that if the deterministic view is inaccurate, urban renewal could be a colossal failure. Alonso argues that urban renewal is based on the assumption that centrifugal expansion of the city will be turned inward as the aging of structures, sequential occupance by different-status residents, and population growth leave the city center open for high-income housing. An analogy is offered by Alonso between this pattern of migration and a convection flow, as in a pot of boiling water. However, if it is lower-density, rather than lower-cost, land that attracts the rich to the suburbs, even at a cost of accessibility, and if this were generally true, then if a whole city developed so quickly that its structures did not have time to age and deteriorate, one would still find that through the working out of tastes, costs, and income in the structure of the market, the city would stilll show the same basic urban form: low income near the center, high income farther out. Urban renewal cannot provide low densities at the center of the city. The land value is too high. Alonso surmises that if his argument is an accurate portrayal of reality, a change in the nature of the demand for space and privacy would be needed to avert the possibility of large-scale failure of urban renewal.

Firey's contention that values determine land use is different from the deterministic and supraindividual social-force theories of, for example, Burgess and Hoyt, in that it proposes that culturally based decisions, rather than, or even opposite from, economic or logistical calculations, will determine structure. For deterministic theories to subsume Firey's cultural variable, deterministic factors of exchange in the urban-space market would need to be expanded to include more-than-obvious economic considerations. Loss of parsimony and general applicability might be a cost of such a tactic, but it is within the limits of the logic of the deterministic framework. Indeed, application of cultural factors to neighborhood choice and structure has been a focus of one vein of study in race relations, an example of which is Hawley and Rock's (1973) collection of papers on racial and socioeconomic factors in choice of housing.

Lee (1978b) suggests that Firey's symbolic ecology may have worked in reverse in relation to Skid Row. The area's bad reputation made it the easy target of social planners before natural, deterministic factors might have led to the present state of its physical demise, if ever. This suggests that Skid Row may have been prematurely dispersed, that as a subculture it may well have the collective strength to invade another area, and that the very same negative cultural values associated with Skid Row that led to its physical demise may allow it to successfully invade another area since invasion by a low-status group is aided or allowed by the evacuation of residents of the invaded area.

Social Engineering. Lynch and Rodwin (1958), according to Chapin (1971), discuss the formulation of goals and the planner's task in efforts aimed at shaping future urban form with the goals that have been identified. Lynch and Rodwin hold that goals should to some extent reflect the democratic process and essentially have, first, a human basis and, second, an economic one, maximizing return and minimizing cost in both a social and economic sense. The relevance of this work for the present effort is its focus on goals. This focus assumes that human volition is, or theoretically can be, a determining variable in urban rearrangement, if not development. This implementation of goals, or volition, may be termed *social engineering*.

Broadly speaking, social engineering may be conceived of as any use of social power, any case in which people are made to act in a way they would not act were it not for some outside source of volition. A perhaps more-limited and -useful meaning of social engineering would refer to decisions that involve large numbers or whole categories of persons. If a theory of social engineering exists, it might be that it is possible and desirable to implement socially desirable values and goals through the manipulation of people and events. The doctrine of laissez faire is perhaps the diametric opposite. Social engineering is like physical engineering in that a problem is identified, solutions and contingencies are discussed and planned for, laborers are hired, materials are procured and manipulated, and the outcome is more-or-less evident. For example, Adolph Hitler practiced bad social engineering; Franklin D. Roosevelt practiced good social engineering. (Both of these statements have been debated.) It will not do to condemn all social engineering because a politician falls into disgrace any more than it is sensible to condemn the field of civil engineering when a bridge falls into the river. The political process is in large part social engineering. Law and the democratic process ideally act to screen out bad social engineering.

Skid Row appears to have been the victim, or the beneficiary, of social engineering. We can test the efficacy of social engineering by comparing the outcome with the specifications. The plan, or blueprint, involved in the Skid Row–elimination project is most fully explicated by Bogue (1963), as reviewed in the previous chapter. He saw as a desirable goal the elimination of Skid Row, as did Plunkert (1961), Plaut (1967), and Nimmer (1972).

Buildings were to be demolished or renovated, and men were to be rehabilitated and/or cared for in treatment programs. The Federal Housing Act of 1949, made possible by a coalition of business and social-welfare interests, created the Urban Renewal Agency, the vehicle making the Skid Row plan possible.

While urban renewal initially focused on decent housing for all, much or most of its effort has been directed at demolition in areas adjacent to CDBs, always including Skid Row. This fact scores against the efficacy of social engineering. The direction of the plan changed. The goals of Bogue and other social planners score well in the demolition phase of the project but more poorly in rehabilitation, at least according to the findings of Fagan and Mauss (1978). That Skid Row could be eliminated or made to disappear seems an overly ambitious goal, but it is an empirical question that we judge in the next chapters.

The desirability of the plans to eliminate Skid Row clearly involves value judgment. Different views might well form different opinions. Hopefully, social engineers do attempt to bring to bear humane ethical ideals such as Jefferson's "right to life, liberty, and the pursuit of happiness"; or the Golden Rule, "Do unto others as you would have others do unto you"; or Bentham's "greatest good for the greatest number"; or Kant's dictum, "If a behavior is right in every situation, then it is right behavior." However, we will not be able to make a definitive judgment about how these bear on the social engineering imposed on Skid Row. Suffice it to say that the coercive rehabilitation proposed by Bogue has not been successfully implemented to this author's knowledge.

Conclusion

Obviously, by the number and variety of more-or-less-predictive models, the pattern of urban spatial structure is characterized by complexity and variety. Generalizations naturally fail to include all factors involved. Table 2-1 is an attempt to summarize the positions reviewed thus far. The theories and perspectives reviewed in this chapter vary in the degree to which they are relevant to Skid Row. Also varying is the extent to which the hypotheses implied by the theories are directly implied. Therefore, as an aid in arriving at some idea of what the strongest hypotheses are, table 2-2 shows an assessment of the relative strength of each of the hypotheses based on the relevance of the theories to Skid Row's location and on the directness with which the theory implies the hypothesis. A simple sum of the relevance and directness ratings provides a rank ordering of the hypotheses. This sum is shown in the far right column of table 2-2. The best bet appears to be that Skid Row will gradually disappear, according to the theories reviewed. A

Table 2-1
Summaries of Theories and Their Predictions of Skid Row Location
Following Dispersal

Theorist or Theory	Summary	Prediction
Quinn	Functional importance determines ability to occupy location median to required services.	(1) To the degree Skid Row has lost functional importance, it will be dispersed. The area may disappear as a distinct niche in the urban mosaic. (2) Clusters of small Skid Row areas will center around locations median to remaining services.
Hawley on natural area	Human behavior reflects its surroundings.	If the dinginess of Skid Row is cleaned up, the behavior characteristic of Skid Row will disappear. Skid Row may thus become imperceptible.
Hawley on symbiosis	Symbiotic units appear together.	Missions and Skid Row men have a symbiotic relationship: Where there are missions there will be Skid Row men. Skid Row qualities will vary positively with number of missions.
Burgess	City develops in concentric zones around the CBD. higher-status districts are farther out. The area of homeless men is adjacent to the CBD.	Skid Row will remain adjacent to the CBD in buildings suffering from lack of maintenance. A shift is possible to any quadrant around the CBD.
Hoyt	City develops in radiating sectors usually corresponding to traffic arteries. Status of residents of a sector tends to be uniform. Low-status sectors tend to be far from high-status sectors and on low ground, near transportation or industrial facilities.	Skid Row will move farther from the CBD, probably in same sector, not uphill, probably along railroad tracks or waterfront.
Harris	City develops around nuclei away from the CDB as well as around the CDB.	Location of satellite Skid Row areas around older communities engulfed by city is possible.

Table 2-1 continued

Theorist or Theory	Summary	Prediction
Stouffer	Opportunities close in will prevent migration over a distance. More opportunities at a distance will influence longer-distance migration.	Skid Row will remain in CBD but gradually disperse as opportunities dwindle .
Brown and Moore	Locations of vacancies discovered through interpersonal communications are limited to the awareness spaces of acquaintances.	Skid Row will remain close to present location but disperse gradually as housing diminishes.
Hawley on communication preceding migration	Pioneers precede mass movements.	Because Schmid identifies two outlying areas in Seattle where men with Skid Row addresses were arrested for drunkenness, satellite Skid Row formation is indicated.
Rose	Racial invasion triggers the moving out of the invaded, thus implementing succession.	Skid Row's low status could allow it to move, relatively intact, to another area.
Roebuck	Clearing the slum does not make the poor go away permanently. They move to the next least expensive area.	Skid Row, as a segment of the population of the poor, will move to the next cheapest area, near the CBD, probably; in satellite Skid Rows; or in cities or towns of the hinterland.
Cooley	Transportation costs determine rents.	Marginal utilization of land by Skid Row institutions will be reduced. Only profitable institutions will remain—for example, large missions with salvage operations.
Guttenberg	Distribution of facilities is positively correlated with ease of transportation.	Ease of transportation for Skid Row men is nearly a constant so that Skid Row will not expand in size beyond its present dimensions.
Firey	Cultural values determine land use.	The negative cultural value of Skid Row made it an

Table 2-1 continued

Theorists or Theory	Summary	Prediction
		easy mark for planners of demolition, but the same negative cultural value associated with Skid Row will repel others in a new area and allow Skid Row to move to another area through the process of invasion and succession.
Social engineering	People can be manipulated when desirable to do so. Skid Row is undesirable. It should be eliminated. Demolish the buildings or renovate them, and rehabilitate the men.	Skid Row will be eliminated through demolition or renovation of buildings and relocation and cure of Skid Row men.

Table 2-2
Cumulation of Hypotheses

Hypothesis	Predicting Theory	Relevancy Rating	Directness Rating	Rating Sum	Sum Total
Disapperance of Skid Row as distinct area	Quinn	2 (high)	1 (low)	3	
	Hawley on natural area	2	1	3	
	Social engineering	2	2	4	10
Gradual dispersal	Quinn	2	2	4	
	Hawley on symbiosis	2	2	4	
	Stouffer	2	2	4	
	Brown and Moore	2	2	4	
	Cooley	2	1	3	19
Relatively intact shift to similar distinct area	Burgess	1	2	3	
	Hoyt	1	2	3	
	Rose	1	2	3	
	Roebuck	1	2	3	
	Firey	1	1	2	14

Table 2–2 continued

Hypothesis	Predicting Theory	Relevance Rating	Directness Rating	Rating Sum	Sum Total
Partial dispersal to satellite Skid Rows	Harris and Ullman	1	1	2	
	Hawley on advance communication	1	1	2	
	Roebuck	1	1	2	6
Partial dispersal to hinterland Skid Rows	Roebuck	1	1	2	2

close second choice appears to be that Skid Row will shift relatively intact to another area near the CDB. However, each of the theories predicting an intact shift is of low relevancy to Skid Row. Gradual dispersion is implied by four theories relevant to Skid Row. The third-ranking alternative, predicted by three theories relevant to Skid Row, is its disappearance as a unique area. Partial dispersal to satellite Skid Rows ranks a distant fourth, and partial dispersal to the hinterland is the least likely alternative predicted by the theories reviewed.

All of the variables influencing Skid Row men's behavior are going to influence different numbers of men in different directions. The figures in the righthand column may be taken as predictions of the attraction strength of the various options that displaced skid row men collectively have. In chapter 3, the data sources we draw upon to determine these vectors are explained. In chapter 4, the findings are presented. In chapter 5, we reflect on the theories with a view from the data.

3

Documenting in
Loving Detail

Qualitative analysts ask such questions as: What kinds of things are going on here? What are the forms of this phenomenon? What variations do we find in this phenomenon? That is, qualitative analysis is addressed to the task of delineating forms, kinds, and types of social phenomena; of documenting in loving detail the things that exist.

—Lofland (1971, p. 13)

Skid Row is many things to many people, but descriptions of the area portray a relatively distinct picture. However, concentrations of Skid Row are nowadays only roughly marked by readily recognizable features. Even some photographs of Skid Row (Bogue 1963; Bahr 1973) might not appear other than off-the-main-track commercial streets to one not cued that Skid Row was the subject of the pictures. Therefore, the measurement of Skid Row attempted in this work has included as many aspects of the meaning of Skid Row as could be practicably applied. Several behaviors and institutions associated with the disaffiliation, alcohol consumption, and poverty of Skid Row are examined over varying numbers of years to meaningfully measure Skid Row and the pattern of its existence.

The Skid Row-ness Scale

The principal and most direct measurement instrument is a scale, shown in table 3-1, composed of Skid Row qualities and applied in a physical inspection of Skid Row and possible emergent Skid Row areas. The Skid Row-ness-scale items were chosen following a review of literature and two months of the author's living in and near Seattle's Skid Row area. The scale items reflect much of the Skid Row life-style. The list of scale items was used as an observation guide in areas including nearly 200 blocks over a seven-year period. The purpose of the scale was to measure and describe the gradient of Skid Row as a physical area and as a subcultural area. Each item on the scale is assigned a weight based on the centrality of the item to the meaning of Skid Row. Items rating a 3 are sine qua non characteristics of Skid Row and are seldom, if ever, found anywhere but on Skid Row. Items rating a 2 are primarily Skid Row features but are also found elsewhere

47

Table 3–1
The Skid Row–ness Scale and Ratings of the Centrality of Each Scale Item to Skid Row

Scale Items	Centrality Rating (1 = low, 3 = high)
Loiterers, standing and sitting	1
Recumbant loiteres	2
Derelicts	2
Unbroken discarded bottles	1
Bottle gangs	3
Secondhand stores	3
Missions	3
Hotels, depending on charge for a room	3, 2, or 1
Cafés, depending on prices	2 or 1
Taverns, depending on price of a pint of wine	2 or 1
Pawn shops	2
Plasma-collection centers	1
Barber schools	2
Casual-labor offices	3

and are items that not every Skid Row area necessarily includes. Items rating a 1 are more common on Skid Row than elsewhere. The scale is composed of both transitory items and institutions. The scale is intended to be simply additive. The higher the sum of rating points, the higher degree or level of Skid Row–ness. The face validity of the items, the ratings, and the scale as a whole is the issue in the following section.

Scale Items

The first five items in table 3–1 are the transitory items, and the last nine are the institutions. Each item is defined and discussed, and the centrality weight of each is justified. *Loiterers, standing and sitting,* are people outside buildings in public places, not moving, and not obviously waiting for a bus or taxi or conducting other business. People in automobiles or in a sidewalk cafe are not included. No one near a bus stop or near the curb looking up and down the street as if waiting for a taxi or other ride is counted. Workers, (for example, street, sewer, or telephone workers) who commonly work outside and might be considered to be loitering when waiting for the next thing to do on their job or when taking coffee breaks were not counted. Loiterers rate one centrality point because Skid Row men often do little more than loiter. Most are unemployed and lack discretionary money for diversions that would take them off the sidewalk. Loiterers rate only one point because loitering is not unusual elsewhere. The only place known to the author where loitering is nearly as common as it is on Skid Row is in urban black neighborhoods on some commercial streets, especially at night. Loiterers in parks and public squares pose a problem. Many loiterers in these places are Skid Row men, but many are probably shoppers or people waiting for shoppers. Nevertheless, they are all counted as loiterers. That this adds somewhat inordinately to the measurement of Skid Row-ness is taken into account in the analysis of the findings.

Recumbant loiterers, classically lying in the gutter, though usually lying elsewhere, represent the epitome of the stereotype of Skid Row. This behavior—on sidewalks, in doorways, parks, alleys, and other places—is common on Skid Row, not only because of drunkenness or the aftermath of drunkenness but also because of lack of a place to spend the night. Under these circumstances, one can stay warm at night by keeping on the move and sleep somewhere in the sun the next day. Recumbant loiterers rate two centrality points. They do not merit three points only because people do lie on the ground elsewhere, and men are not always lying on the ground on Skid Row.

Derelicts also epitomize Skid Row. They are usually unkempt men who shave irregularly, walk irregularly, and have sallow, unhealthy-appearing skin. Sometimes wine sores are visible. The poor diet characteristic of heavy drinkers retards healing. Minor cuts and scrapes, something the staggering drunk is prone to incur, fail to heal and tend to fester in a characteristic way. Younger Skid Row men, who are derelicts in the same sense that the word is applied to older Skid Row men, may not have such badly deteriorated health, but classification of them into the derelict category is usually possible anyway. They tend to dress peculiarly, often wearing heavy shirts (three or more sometimes), heavy shoes, and poorly fitting pants. They get their clothes at missions, and if they are not sleeping in a room where they can leave their things, they wear all the clothes they currently own. If it gets too hot they simply discard the extra clothing, only to get more when needed. It is not at all uncommon to see discarded clothing on Skid Row. It is often easier to discard clothing and get more than to wash present clothing. Orwell comments on another way of identifying this classic breed:

> [O]ne would have known him for a tramp a hundred yards away. There was something in his drifting style of walk, and the way he had of hunching his shoulders forward, essentially abject. Seeing him walk, you felt instinctively that he would sooner take a blow than give one. [1933, p. 150]

Care was taken to classify a man as a derelict only if he manifested multiple derelict characteristics. Derelicts rate two centrality points. They do not merit three because unhealthy, unkempt people exist elsewhere. They rate more than one because they do tend to confine themselves to Skid Row. Occasionally, one is seen in the CBD, where he looks woefully out of place. They thus pass their time on Skid Row.

Unbroken discarded bottles usually reflect recent drinking in doorways, alleys, and other more-or-less-visible public places. Nonalcoholic-beverage bottles do not count. Broken bottles are often impossible to count. The number of discarded bottles is a conservative measurement of Skid Row–ness (to the extent that Skid Row–ness involves drinking) in that, first, those who can afford tavern drinking usually do not drink on the street and, second, in Seattle at least, bottles do not tend to accumulate. City employees pick up discarded bottles and other rubbish on a more-or-less-regular basis. One man was retained by the city of Seattle in 1974 primarily to pick up refuse (bottles) in the Skid Row are. Hired midway in this study, we shall see what difference he made. Unbroken discarded bottles rate one centrality point each. Bottles are discarded in many places by people too lazy to deposit them properly at a recycling center or in a waste receptacle. However, left standing on doorsteps, sidewalks, and in alleys, bottles indicate public drinking, and that is very typical of Skid Row.

Bottle gangs are groups of Skid Row drinkers who pool their change and send one of their more-or-less-respectable members to "make a run" for (another) jug. Wallace identifies the centrality of the bottle gang to Skid Row:

> To be completely acculturated in Skid Row subculture is to be a drunk— since Skid Rowers place strong emphasis on group drinking and the accul- turated person is by definition a conformist. The drunk has rejected every single one of society's established values and wholly conforms to the basic values of Skid Row subculture. Food, shelter, employment, appearance, health, and all other considerations are suboriented by the drunk to the group's need for alcohol. This group constitutes the drunk's total social world, and it in turn bestows upon him any status, acceptance, or security he may possess.

> [Such] heavy drinking is a product of group behavior patterns rather than the result of individual cravings for alcohol. [1965, pp. 181–182, 184]

Drinking in bottle gangs is matched as a pastime only by the process or organizing a bottle gang. Norms regulating the situation include congeniality, politeness, and not "hogging the bottle." While Skid Row means much more than drinking, and since many people living in Skid Row areas are certainly not alcoholics (and some are even teetotalers), a bottle gang rates three centrality points. The visible occurrence of alcohol consumption in this manner is unique in the urban world to Skid Row.

These items vary in number easily from time to time and block to block.

The following are more-permanent factors, the institutions of Skid Row. *Secondhand stores* are part of Skid Row for two reasons. First, they provide Skid Row men with cheap or free but often sturdy clothes, shoes, and overcoats. The plea that one has no money but great need is usually sufficient to reduce the marked price to free. Second, Skid Row men are usually the people who solicit and process the donated merchandise sold in these stores. When men live in the missions, this is the work they do. For this reason especially, secondhand stores rate three centrality points. Secondhand stores are just barely a three-point item because they do exist elsewhere, usually in or near poor neighborhoods, but they are most common to Skid Row. Furthermore, Skid Row could not exist as it does without the secondhand stores. They support the big missions that provide lodging.

Missions are most highly central to Skid Row. They exist nowhere else and Skid Row would be hard put to exist without them. They provide free meals one can count on. Some provide employment and some provide shelter, three nights for free and $.75 to $2.00 per night after that for accommodations ranging from a cot among 100 or more cots in a warehouselike room to a single room with a sink. The missions also provide an avenue out of Skid Row for those who wish to take advantage of it. The religious function of the missions is a matter of serious question. While the number of men professing to want to be saved has been by no means small over the years, any observer in a typical Skid Row mission service will note that the overwhelming majority of those in attendance usually pay remarkably little attention to the service. A curious, almost contractual, feature of the relationship between the mission and the Skid Row man is the consistent length of the service. At the end of one hour, more or less precisely, if the service is not obviously drawing to a close, a distinct rise in the chapel's noise level may be distinguished, caused by coughing and shuffling of feet, that informs a long-winded preacher that the service has run its course. In contrast to the apathy during the service, close attention is paid to the refreshments served afterwards. Pockets and bags are filled with leftovers. Naturally, missions rate three centrality points.

Hotels renting a nightly room for $2.25 per night or under in 1972 in Seattle rate three centrality points. Those charging from $2.26 to $3.00 per night rate two centrality points. Those from $3.01 to $4.00 per night rate one centrality point, and those charging over $4.00 per night do not indicate Skid Row–ness. If nightly rates were not available, they were extrapolated from weekly or monthly rates based on comparison with hotels offering both nightly and longer-term rates. Hotels were priced only in 1972, and the hotel, if it remained open and if no obvious changes were observed, retained its original rating for the course of the study. Cheap hotels are found on every Skid Row, and nowhere else are hotels found with the qualities of Skid Row hotels. Absolutely threadbare carpets, two metal garbage cans at the head of the stairs on each floor, incredibly filthy, half-rotted-away gauze curtains adorning hall windows, and two toilets and one shower per floor were included for the nightly fare of $1.80 in 1972. The room was clean; the bed was uncomfortable. There are no so-called cage hotels in Seattle. A cage is a five-foot by eight-foot room with the walls extending from about six inches off the floor up seven feet to a chicken-wire ceiling, for ventilation. The typical Skid Row hotel occupies the floors above a commercial establishment in a four-to-eight-story building. Hotels are a significant part of the lives of some Skid Row men even if they do not live in them. Occupants sometimes share rooms, and hotel clerks frequently call the police to remove the loiterers, which gains for the Skid Row man the roof over his head he was hoping for in loitering around the hotel looking for a friend to share a room.

Cafés with a combination breakfast of meat, two eggs, hash-brown potatoes, toast, and coffee, or roughly the equivalent, for $.95 or less in 1972 in Seattle rated two points. The same breakfast for $.96 to $1.15 rated one point. This scale was based on a comparison of Skid Row and off–Skid Row eating places in Seattle in August 1972. The contents of the meal were chosen as the comparison unit because it was a more-or-less-typical breakfast menu. As with hotels, café price ratings were given only in 1972 and remained the same for the institution if it remained open, unless obvious renovation occurred. Cafés opening after 1972 were rated on the basis of appearance. Skid Row cafes of long standing tend to have a dingy, smoke-and-grease-coated atmosphere. Newer establishments catering to the Skid Row trade lack this atmosphere but have older equipment, a Skid Row–appearing clientele, and Skid Row–appearing help. There are very few newer Skid Row–type cafés, but there are inexpensive cafés elsewhere.

Taverns with the least expensive pint of wine selling for $.75 or less in 1972 in Seattle rated two points, and those pricing the cheapest pint of wine from $.76 to $.90 rate one point. Wine in Washington has more alcohol per dollar cost than any other drink, and it is by far the most popular drink on Skid Row. The price of a pint was chosen because it is the lowest priced quantity available and because a pint bottle will fit in a hip or coat pocket. This is an important consideration when public consumption is banned but planned. Being in public possession of a liquor bottle and having it observed by a police officer can result in the contents' being poured out, or sometimes arrest. Furthermore, the price of a pint of wine is a relevant measure of Skid Row–ness because this price in some cases distinguishes between taverns that welcome Skid Row men and those that do not. Although licensing in the state of Washington permits it, many taverns do not sell wine by the bottle, and many do not sell pints. While no exact tabulation was made of the discarded unbroken bottles observed in alleys, doorways, and elsewhere, perhaps 90 percent were wine bottles, and about half of these were pints. Liquor stores and grocery stores selling wine were also counted. Although these stores do not fit the strict criteria for classifying Skid Row–ness items, because of the centrality of drinking to Skid Row men, these establishments are counted as institutions serving Skid Row. Especially in developing Skid Row areas, they could be focal points of new Skid Row development. As with hotels and cafés, the original rating of a tavern was used throughout the study unless significant changes were apparent.

Pawn shops, or loan establishments displaying merchandise left as collateral, unclaimed, and for sale, cater to marginal Skid Row men—that is, marginal on the high-status end of the range of Skid Row men. Orwell (1933) provides a colorful description of the role of the pawn shop in the life of the down and out in Paris. Its place in contemporary U.S. Skid Row life is less central, however. U.S. Pawn shops usually deal in fairly high-priced items by Skid Row standards. However, pawn shops are on every Skid Row or near it, and they are not usually located elsewhere. The same attraction that brings people and other institutions to Skid Row brings pawn shops— namely, low rent. So, should pawn shops move, Skid Row could be close by. Since they are not central to the Skid Row life-style, at least anymore, pawn shops rate two centrality points.

Plasma-collection centers (blood banks) paid $5.00 for a pint of blood in 1972 in Seattle and Tacoma. In 1974, national publicity focused on the inordinate number of cases of hepatitis and other diseases that apparently had been transmitted through blood transfusions. A proposed ban on paying for blood would have curbed a standard procedure on Skid Row for raising capital for a jug. Plasma-collection centers are also located away from Skid Row, but because the Skid Row literature cited them and because there is one in Seattle on Skid Road, a plasma-collection center rates one centrality point. Interestingly enough, during the course of the study, the one plasma-collection center on Skid Road in Seattle moved four blocks, and a new one appeared on Skid Row in Tacoma.

Barber schools are typical of Skid Row. They offer more-or-less-professional haircuts at a fraction of professional costs or for free. While fairly often appearing unkempt, even the low-status wino/derelict usually does not have very long hair. He occasionally affords or bargains for that modicum of self-respect a haircut might impart. Some men report that short hair keeps scalp problems at a minimum. A barger college on Seattle's First Avenue charged $1.25 in 1972 for a haircut, in contrast to the $1.75 price in a shop three blocks away. Arrangements could be, and often were, made for free haircuts. Barber schools are located other than on Skid Row but are typically on or near Skid Row. They thus rate two centrality points.

Casual-labor offices are the final item on the Skid Row–ness scale. Having had a much greater function on Skid Row in the past, these institutions still thrive, though in smaller numbers. In the West they offer agricultural jobs in season and industrial odd jobs year round. Transportation is usually furnished by the employer on out-of-town jobs. On in-town jobs payment is daily or weekly depending on the labor-office practice. These establishments have always and still do exist on Skid Row and nowhere else. Other types of employment agencies are not distinguished by their large bare rooms and straight wooden benches, as is the typical casual-labor office. They rate three centrality points each.

Other Items

Several other items were considered for inclusion on the scale but for various reasons were not. The item *women* was included on the scale at a negative-one centrality point, but as Skid Row was invaded by renovation and the accompanying office staffs and other business personnel, the number of women on a block became so great at times as to result in a negative Skid Row–ness total even when there were several positive Skid Row–ness items. Women were thus omitted from the tabulation. The absence of women has been a characteristic of Skid Row historically. Bahr (1973, pp. 175–221), reporting on one of the few studies of homeless women, writes that Skid Row women are rare. There are many homeless women, but they are not geographically concentrated and tend to remain sequestered in hotels.

Number of times panhandled per block was considered as a scale item but was dropped as the author became more "street wise" and did not attract panhandlers. Begging for money on one pretense or another is characteristic of a minority of Skid Row men, but those who engage in this practice are occasionally very active at it.

Theaters showing sex movies exclusively, all-night theaters, and *penny arcades* each are found on or near Skid Row but were not included on the scale. Each caters to the urban population of single men, but older, obvious Skid Row types are usually not welcome patrons, and they are not usually seen in these institutions.

Skid Rows are usually adjacent to *waterfronts* and/or railroad tracks. Distance from these facilities was considered as a scale item, but it was not used because of near uniformity of distance or most Skid Row blocks from them.

Application of the Scale

The areal unit in the application of the Skid Row–ness scale was both sides of the street for the length of one city block. Observations were made at the corner of the block, on either side of the street for the length of the block, in doorways, and in alley entrances to the street. With clipboard in hand, the researcher walked the side of the street that at first glance appeared most likely to provide the best opportunity to observe all scale items present on that block. For example, if one side of a street had three vacant lots and two empty buildings and the other side was a solid block of commercial enterprises, then the researcher would walk on the side with the vacant lots and buildings, focusing attention mainly there but not neglecting to mark down items visible across the street, such as loiterers, names of taverns, and other items. While the unit of analysis could be as small as the length of one city block, the reporting in chapter 4 is mostly done by areas, from four to fifty-four blocks in size.

Observations were all made between 1:00 P.M. and 5:00 P.M., Monday through Friday, in early August each year from 1972 through 1978, seven years in a row. The choice of the month of August, a result of the scheduling of the first summer of the project, had the effect of depressing the total Skid Row-ness count by eliminating those who spend only winter in the Skid Row area. The choice of afternoons was made to exclude workingpeople, while still giving the day a chance to warm up, allowing men to be outside.

Police Department Data

The second data source bearing on the question of Skid Row relocation is the records of the Seattle Police Department. Seattle arrest files were made available for the period 1973 through 1976 through the cooperation of the management-information and data-processing staff of the Seattle Police Department and through the efforts of researchers at Washington State University (Fagan and Mauss 1978).

Arrest Rates

Arrest rates by census tract for offenses typical of Skid Row men for these four years provide a partial picture of the locations of certain typical Skid Row activities. Figures clearly include more offenders than might be classified as typical of Skid Row, but just as clearly, Skid Row men do not all get booked for all of their illegal activities. Charges typical of Skid Row in Seattle are unlawful disposition of liquor, disturbing the peace, begging, trespassing, and urinating in public.

"Rap Sheets"

Individual arrest files ("rap sheets") identified by internal identification number only and containing no names, make possible the locating of the illegal behaviors (which have come to the attention of the Seattle police) of a number of persons who can be identified with Skid Row. Following these persons' paths through their "rap sheets" gives an indication of where Skid Row is, to the extent that these offenders are inhabitants of Skid Row. To acquire a typical Skid Row group, the records of 250 persons who were charged with a typical Skid Row offense in a Skid Row census tract in 1973, the first year data were available, were randomly selected from the thousands of possible such records. There were 12,032 Skid Row–type offenses in 1973 charged to an undetermined number of persons in the Seattle Skid Row census tracts. The number 250 was chosen as a substantial yet manageable sample, likely to yield the desired information—namely, where Skid Row men go from Skid Row.

Census Data

Census data provide a long-range perspective the other data sources do not. Examination of 1950, 1960, and 1970 census material most relevant to Skid Row shows relative change in the areas other data sources cover and in a few more areas as well. Five characteristics of Skid Row available by census tract in published census data are (1) sex ratio, (2) median number of persons per household, (3) percentage of renter-occupied housing units, (4) percentage of city median rent averaged in the census tract, and (5) percentage of men 14 years old or older not in the labor force. The census tracts roughly correspond to (in all cases are larger than) the areas identified as distinct for purposes of applying the Skid Row–ness scale. Census tracts correspond exactly to Seattle Police Department tracts.

Detox

Beginning 1 January 1975, the Seattle Police Department officially began phasing out the handling of public drunkenness. Civilian patrols took over the job, picking up patients for the Seattle Alcohol Treatment Facility, Detox (Fagan and Mauss 1978). The Detox pickup procedure, unlike police apprehension, requires the consent of the prospective patient. After this initial contact, a screening procedure determines if admission to Detox is appropriate. Five out of six patients screened are admitted. After a typical stay of under three days, each patient is referred to a long-term alcohol-treatment program. Although Detox is open to all, but is not free to other than the indigent, the initial twenty-seven months operation primarily served patients who were typical of Skid Row. This was shown to be the case by Fagan and Mauss (1978) through comparison of sociodemographic variables listed in Skid Row rescue-mission files and on Detox intake forms. Detox appears to be the implementation of the overall plan of those people who have suggested Skid Row can and should be eliminated, and it is examined in that light.

Skid Row Interviews

In 1973, as part of a multifaceted research project dealing with alcohol-rehabilitation programs, Skid Row missions, and Skid Row ecology (this work), 117 interviews were conducted in the Seattle Skid Road area with men who can more or less be considered Skid Row men. At least most of them lived in the Skid Road area or near there. The question directly relevant to this study, "Where do you think most guys living around here will go if the older hotels (for example, the Puget Sound Hotel) keep getting closed up? [Probe for at least one specific place]," provides perceptual data from Skid Row people themselves on their expected destination following dispersal.

The sample for this study was gathered in a rather unique way, termed early in the project the watering-hole-sampling technique. Men were buttonholed in parks, public squares, and on the street (40 percent); in restaurants (16 percent); at the First Avenue Service Center, a place Skid Row men and other unemployed people pass time with free coffee, reading material, and games (17 percent); in missions (12 percent); and in various other locations where "street people" hang out. As Wolfe described the technique:

> While this [sampling procedure] in no way represents a random sampling of animals [or people], it does give the scientist access to an "opportunistic" sample having no *known* or *a priori* biases. [1977, p. 47]

It became apparent, though, that the interviewers inserted definite bias into the sampling procedure. One of the interviewers (this author) selected out (70 of the 117 interviews) what he thought to be a fair range of Skid Row men, from drunken derelicts who were difficult to interview to dignified retirees, essentially anyone that looked approachable, but with a definite bias toward men of the not-too-far-gone-derelict type. The other principal interviewer (31 interviews), a female year-long resident of the Seattle Skid Road area, selected more of an upper-crust Skid Row sample. With 16 interviews by others, in all, the sample is probably loosely representative of Skid Row. The responses of this sample are valuable as the only data source projecting into the future.

Potters Field Burials

A final source of data offering information about the changing location of
Skid Row in Seattle is the King County Medical Examiner's records. These
records list the addresses of those dying in Seattle without known relatives.
This means that no person claimed the body, which therefore has to be
buried at public expense. The characteristic of disaffiliation so typical of
Skid Row men (Bahr 1973) is epitomized in these death records. Comparison of 1971–1972 data with 1977–1978 data shows potentially important
shifts in the Skid Row, to the extent that disaffiliation is characteristic of
Skid Row.

A Similar Effort

From the time of the inception of this study until after the last round of data
collection in 1978, this type of objective measurement of Skid Row was
thought to be unique. As it turns out, Blumberg, Shipley, and Barsky (1978)
attempted a similar procedure in order to locate emergent Skid Rows in
Philadelphia. The indicators used by Blumberg and his associates were
presence of bottle gangs, police records of typical Skid Row offenses, neighborhood real estate characteristics, and long-term real estate trends.

For several reasons, each of these indicators was deemed less than
useful by Blumberg and his co-workers. They learned that bottle gangs
existed in areas of Philadelphia other than Skid Row, though bottle gangs
outside Skid Row, according to Blumberg's informants, tended to have
stable memberships while those in Skid Row areas were temporary groups.
Blumberg did not attempt to directly observe bottle gangs but observed
accumulations of bottles. Police data on reported crimes and arrests were
seen as deficient because they might indicate efforts to maintain
neighborhood quality rather than an actual increase in Skid Row characteristics. The crimes Blumberg, Shipley, and Barsky considered were drunkenness, vagrancy, and disorderly conduct. In relation to neighborhood real
estate characteristics, the Blumberg group thought about interviewing people in the real estate business but did not because they felt the measurement
was too obtrusive and could actually cause change. They felt that even
simply questioning real estate people about Skid Row characteristics could
alter land values and property-maintenance practices. Real estate trends, as
measured by patterns of tax assessment from 1912 to the present, were
found problematic as well. On one hand, the city policy of maintaining the
stability of assessed values of property prevented meaningful comparisons
over time. Additionally, Blumberg and his associates discovered a complex
process of real estate trends in potential and incipient Skid Row areas. As

an area deteriorates, land values do decline, but when conversion to cheap rooming houses takes place, building values rise in the midst of a blighted area.

In summarizing their efforts in using objective measurement, based on known characteristics of Skid Row, for the purpose of testing predictions of new skid row locations, Blumberg, Shipley, and Barsky acknowledge that specific reasons caused each measurement procedure to be ineffective. However, they are critical of their overall efforts as well. They state that it seems likely that more-comprehensive urban trends than a shift in Skid Row itself made their predictions of emergent Skid Row locations naive and unrealistic in the first place.

Conclusion

That broad urban trends exist is certainly true. Nevertheless, Skid Row as an urban entity has persisted quite intact through trends in the past, and it may well continue. Its location is of continuing interest, and predictions—naive or otherwise—are certainly not out of order. While each measurement effort has its limitations, in this study as well as in Blumberg, Shipley, and Barsky's, we should hope that the multiple direct measures used in this study are more valid than those attempted by Blumberg and his associates and that the multiplicity of measures does allow for a valid assessment of Skid Row location.

4 Not Dice

God does not play dice.

—Albert Einstein

This chapter contains the findings of our many observations of the various aspects of Skid Row. Following is a brief review of the data forms used in this study and the relevance and importance of each. First, the street observations of fourteen items that largely define Skid Row, made yearly in early August from 1972 through 1978, are a direct measurement of Skid Row-ness in an area of about 180 blocks known to contain Skid Row characteristics, or blocks adjacent to these. Second, covering a four-year period in the middle of the seven years of street observations is the Seattle Police Department data set, official records that provide aggregate arrest data for Skid Row offenses in selected police districts and four-year "rap sheets" of offenders charged with a Skid Row offense in a Skid Row area in 1973, the first year the data set covers. Variations in this police data set are clearly measures of something other than variations in Skid Row. However, this data set does generate unique and interesting observations about Skid Row and its relations with its environment. Third, a precise and valid spatial measurement of one characteristic of Skid Row, disaffiliation, is contained in the records of the King County Medical Examiner. These records include addresses of people who died in Seattle with no relative or other individual coming forward to arrange a burial. Fourth, the U.S. Census Bureau findings are a meticulously collected set of data providing information about population characteristics and housing for the entire population by census tract, including the census tracts of Skid Row. Data examined were gathered in 1950, 1960, and 1970 in the census tracts that include Skid Row areas, adjacent areas, and possible emerging Skid Row areas. The primary limitation of the census for purposes of examining changes in Skid Row is that data collection only occurs once every ten years. The census does, however, provide a backdrop setting within which to assess the data gathered in the 1970s. Fifth, an examination of the functioning of the Seattle Detox facility to a degree makes possible the evaluation of the implementation of the goals of social engineers. These data demonstrate the extent to which Skid Row has been eliminated through the providing of services and long-term-rehabilitation programs to Skid Row men. Last, responses of

Skid Row-area interviewees—the opinions of the Skid Row men themselves—are the final form of data. The order in which the data sources are
discussed here is the same order as the following presentation. The chapter
concludes with a summary of all findings, and this summary leads into
chapter 5, which reviews the data in light of the predictions inferred from
the theories reviewed in chapter 2.

Street Data

As mentioned in chapter 3, the Skid Row-ness scale was applied to several
areas in Seattle, to the Skid Row area in Tacoma, and to areas in Aberdeen,
Everett, and Bellingham, Washington. In addition, efforts to apply the
scale were made in Bremerton and Mount Vernon, Washington, and Vancouver, British Columbia. Vancouver has an area that has institutions
similar to Skid Row institutions in U.S. cities, but they are far less
segregated from non-Skid Row enterprises than in U.S. cities. This made
the application of the Skid Row-ness scale there difficult and of questionable comparative value. This fact, and the expense and difficulty of traveling to Canada, caused the international comparison to be dropped from the
study. Mount Vernon is a small town (population 10,000), and while it is
theoretically one of the options a displaced Skid Row man has, no real Skid
Row elements exist there except for perhaps a town drunk or two. Bremerton, a short way across Puget Sound from Seattle and a Navy-base town,
thoroughly cleaned up a thriving Skid Row area in the mid-1960s, and scar-
cely a vestige remains. Aberdeen, Everett, and Bellingham (populations
19,000; 52,000; and 41,000 respectively) each has a small but distinct Skid
Row-like area. As in Vancouver, the Skid Row establishments in these
small towns were not clearly segregated. Virtually no change was evident in
two applications of the Skid Row-ness scale, and little was seen as likely or
even possible. The small-city option for Skid Row men driven from the big
city does not seem to be a viable one for noticeably large numbers. This
leaves Tacoma and other areas within Seattle for those who have left the
once large residential Skid Row area around the CBD in Seattle. Table 4-1
identifies the areas observed, the number of blocks each comprises, and the
location of each.

Tacoma is a reasonable destination for Seattle Skid Row men who for
one reason or another leave Seattle's Skid Row. Other cities may attract
many of the displaced, but because the composition of Skid Row is (in addition to transient, sometime laborers and bums) in large part the "home
guard," Tacoma could well become a home base for those displaced from
Seattle. Furthermore, Tacoma was the only city Bahr (1967) found to have a
Skid Row on the rise. Therefore, while the following data essentially pertain

Table 4-1
Street-Observation Areas, Sizes, and Locations

Area	Size	Location
International District	26 blocks	Southeast of the CBD, from Weller Street to Yesler Way, Interstate 5 to Fourth Avenue
Pioneer Square area	54 blocks	South of the CBD, from Fourth Avenue to Western Avenue, King Street to Columbia Street
First Avenue area	37 blocks	West of the CBD, from Columbia Street to Pine Street, Second Avenue to Western Avenue
Belltown	51 blocks	Northwest of the CBD, from Pine Street to Cedar Street, Second Avenue to Western Avenue
Pike Street	4 blocks	East of the CBD, Pike Street only, from Fifth Avenue to Nineth Avenue
Fremont	4 blocks	Two miles north of the CBD, Fremont business district
Ballard	4 blocks	Three-and-one-half miles northwest of the CBD, Ballard Avenue N.W., from N.W. Market Street to Dock Place
Tacoma	9 blocks	Twenty-five miles south of Seattle, east of the Tacoma CBD, near the bus and old train depots.

only to Seattle, the reporting of the street data only includes observations each year from Tacoma along with the observations from areas in Seattle.

The data gathered on the streets of Seattle and Tacoma are, as discussed in chapter 3, divided into two categories—transitory items and institutional items. Transitory items are loiterers, recumbant loiterers, derelicts, discarded bottles, and bottle gangs. Counts on a single block of these items varied as much as from 0 to 20 between one year and the next. Institutional items are secondhand stores, missions, hotels, cafés, taverns, pawn shops, casual-labor offices, barber schools, and blood banks. Recall also from chapter 3 that the items were given point values corresponding to their centrality to Skid Row. The point values of all items together, the grand-total Skid Row-ness scores, are presented by area and year in table 4-2. The point values of the institutional items are presented in table 4-3. The transitory items are then presented in table 4-4, and because the transitory items comprise between 70 and 80 percent of the total Skid Row-ness scores in the various areas, and because they measure change most sensitively, numbers of observations of the three most prominent of them (derelicts, loiterers, and discarded bottles) are shown by area and year in table 4-5, 4-6, and 4-7 respectively. Following this, the grand-total Skid Row-ness scores of certain special categories of blocks are presented by year in table 4-8. The form of tables 4-2, 4-3, and 4-4 is identical. Each cell in these tables contains three figures. The top figure is a score based on the number of observations

Table 4-2
Grand-Total Skid Row-ness Scores, by Year and Area, with Percentages of Yearly Totals and Proportions of 1972 Scores

Area	1972	1973	1974	1975	1976	1977	1978[a]
International	177	190	148	111	132	159	163
District	11	11.3	10.3	8.0	10.7	13.7	12.4
	(1)	(1.07)	(0.84)	(0.63)	(0.75)	(0.90)	(0.92)
Pioneer Square area	661	703	580	547	562	387	608
	41.0	41.7	40.5	39.5	45.4	33.4	46.2
	(1)	(1.06)	(0.88)	(0.83)	(0.85)	(0.59)	(0.92)
First Avenue area	186	204	190	190	98	174	100
	11.5	12.1	13.3	13.7	7.9	15.0	7.6
	(1)	(1.10)	(1.02)	(1.02)	(0.53)	(0.94)	(0.54)
Belltown	330	358	295	328	237	286	333
	20.5	21.2	20.6	23.7	19.1	24.7	25.3
	(1)	(1.08)	(0.89)	(0.99)	(0.72)	(0.87)	(1.01)
Pike Street	39	40	42	34	29	18	14
	2.4	2.4	2.9	2.5	2.3	1.6	1.1
	(1)	(1.03)	(1.08)	(0.87)	(0.74)	(0.46)	(0.36)
Fremont	13	15	15	11	15	19	
	0.8	0.9	1.0	0.8	1.2	1.6	—[b]
	(1)	(1.15)	(1.15)	(0.85)	(1.15)	(1.46)	
Ballard	67	54	48	38	35	29	
	4.2	3.2	3.3	2.7	2.8	2.5	—[b]
	(1)	(0.89)	(0.72)	(0.57)	(0.52)	(0.43)	
Tacoma	140	122	115	125	130	87	97
	8.7	7.2	8.0	9.0	10.5	7.5	7.4
	(1)	(0.87)	(0.82)	(0.89)	(0.93)	(0.62)	(0.69)
Totals	1,613	1,686	1,433	1,384	1,238	1,159	1,315
	100.1[c]	100.0	99.9	99.9	99.9	100.0	100.0
	(1)	(1.05)	(0.89)	(0.86)	(0.77)	(0.72)	(0.82)

Note: In each group of three numbers, the top number indicates the raw score, the middle indicates percentage, and the bottom indicates proportion of 1972 scores.

[a]The 1978 figures are adjusted to include estimates of scores that uncounted blocks would have contributed.

[b]Fremont and Ballard were not covered at all in 1978.

[c]Totals are not all 100.0 % because of rounding.

of the various items multiplied by the point values of each of the items. The middle figure is the percentage of the yearly total of scores of all eight areas. The bottom figure is the proportions of the 1972 score for the particular area. Tables 4-5, 4-6, and 4-7 are the same except, since these tables deal with only one item, the raw number of observations, rather than point value, is reported in the top figure. Table 4-8 is the same as tables 4-2 through 4-4 except categories of blocks other than geographic areas are identified. Certain considerations about the limitations of this data set should be understood by the reader. These are discussed at some length in appendix A. Briefly, fluctuations of a smaller magnitude may be due to the inherent variability of the presence of the objects of study. Gross trends can safely be taken as valid measures of change in Skid Row–ness. With this in mind, let us proceed with an examination of the findings as to where Skid Row went.

Grand Total

The grand-total Skid Row–ness scores shown in table 4–2 clearly show where Skid Row is in Seattle. The Pioneer Square area, the traditional Skid Row, is still the center, with about double the count of the next highest area, Belltown, in all years except 1977. International District and the First Avenue area have substantial counts in the neighborhood of one-fourth the Pioneer Square-area count. The trend evident in the grand-total Skid Row–ness scores is one of gradual decline except for a slight increase in 1973 and a modest increase in 1978. The sharpest declines, by area, have been those in Ballard and on Pike Street. Tacoma shows little decline through 1976 but then drops markedly. The four major Seattle areas each have one or two very low years but seem to pick up the following year, indicating no trend other than gradual decline. Fremont, intitally low, has little room to decline.

Other than decline, the most remarkable pattern in observations of Skid Row behaviors and institutions in the way in which each of the areas seems to hold its own relative to the rest. Allowing for some chance variation, the yearly percentage figures for each of the areas over the years are quite alike. International District, for example, varies in relative contribution to the overall Skid Row–ness total from a low of 8 percent in 1975 to a high of 13.7 percent in 1977, a difference of only 5.7 points. The greatest difference in relative contribution to the total Skid Row–ness score is found in the Pioneer Square area, a difference of 12.8 points between 1977 and 1978. However, if the exceptionally low year of 1977 was not considered, the difference between the highest Pioneer Square-area yearly percentage contribution and the lowest would be only 5.7 points. Incidentally, the reader's confidence in the reliability of this unique Skid Row–ness measure may be enhanced by the relatively small fluctuation in each area's percentage contribution to the yearly Skid Row–ness total as well as by the relative consistency across time of the parenthetical figures in the table. In any case, the total degree of Skid Row–ness in Seattle dropped about 20 percent between 1972 and 1978.

Institutional Items

The institutional-item scores found in table 4–3 show a decline similar to the decline in total Skid Row–ness scores, but with a few notable exceptions.

Table 4-3
Institutional-Item Total Scores, by Year and Area, with Percentages of Yearly Totals and Proportions of 1972 Scores

Area	1972	1973	1974	1975	1976	1977	1978[a]
International	43	42	46	26	29	35	34
District	10.3	10.2	11.9	8.1	9.6	9.9	13.2
	(1)	(0.98)	(1.07)	(0.61)	(0.67)	(0.81)	(0.79)
Pioneer Square area	89	87	76	60	52	78	62
	21.3	21.1	19.6	18.7	17.3	22.2	24.1
	(1)	(0.98)	(0.85)	(0.67)	(0.58)	(0.88)	(0.70)
First Avenue area	69	65	59	47	38	84	37
	16.5	15.7	15.2	14.6	12.6	23.9	14.4
	(1)	(0.94)	(0.86)	(0.68)	(0.55)	(1.22)	(0.54)
Belltown	108	115	108	95	94	73	70
	25.8	27.8	27.8	29.6	31.2	20.7	27.2
	(1)	(1.06)	(1.00)	(0.88)	(0.87)	(0.68)	(0.65)
Pike Street	13	13	12	12	18	18	12
	3.1	3.1	3.1	3.7	6.0	5.1	4.7
	(1)	(1.00)	(0.92)	(0.92)	(1.38)	(1.38)	(0.92)
Fremont	8	10	8	5	5	9	
	1.9	2.4	2.1	1.6	1.7	2.6	—[b]
		(1972 baseline too small for meaningful comparison)					
Ballard	26	23	26	25	22	19	
	6.2	5.6	6.7	7.8	7.3	5.4	—[b]
	(1)	(0.88)	(1.00)	(0.96)	(0.85)	(0.73)	
Tacoma	62	58	53	51	43	36	42
	14.8	14.0	13.6	15.9	14.3	10.2	16.3
	(1)	(0.94)	(0.85)	(0.82)	(0.69)	(0.58)	(0.68)
Totals	418	413	388	321	301	352	257
	99.9[c]	99.9	100.0	100.0	100.0	100.0	99.9
	(1)	(0.99)	(0.93)	(0.77)	(0.72)	(0.84)	(0.61)

Note: In each group of three numbers, the top number indicates the raw score, the middle indicates percentage, and the bottom indicates proportion of 1972 scores.

[a]The 1978 figures are adjusted to include estimates of scores that uncounted blocks would have contributed.

[b]Fremont and Ballard were not covered at all in 1978.

[c]Totals are not all 100.0 % because of rounding.

Because of the nature of the variables, fluctuations are typically not great, but apparently a decline in the number of institutions serving Skid Row in each area has occurred. International District shows some growth in 1977, which is largely the result of the reopening of two hotels. The Pioneer Square area and the First Avenue area both show clear, steady declines except for almost unbelievable gains in 1977. That year the First Avenue area registered a 46-point rise, and the Pioneer Square area showed a

26-point rise. These increases represent increases in the number of taverns, 6 points in each area; cafés, 10 points in the First Avenue area and 4 points in the Pioneer Square area; and pawn shops, secondhand stores, and missions. In regard to missions, each storefront establishment is counted whether it is a multiservice facility offering beds, clothing, meals, religious services, and employment or a smaller facility, perhaps operated by a larger mission and offering only one or a few of these services. This might seem to overrepresent missions in the total count, but the functions they perform (even the small facilities) are central to the concept of Skid Row and therefore qualifies them to be counted. The entrepreneurial spirit, evident in the dramatic increase in institutions especially in the First Avenue area, apparently read the signs of the times wrongly, as is evident in the just as dramatic drop in institutional score between 1977 and 1978. International District saw a rise in institutions serving Skid Row men in 1974 when the three other major areas were registering decreases. The rise there too was followed by a crash. The modest rise in 1977 in International District was maintained in 1978. As opposed to the three other major districts, Belltown takes its biggest drop in institutional-item scores in 1977. Pike Street, Ballard, and Fremont, relatively quite low to begin with, remain that way. Tacoma shows the steadiest pattern of decline in institutional items, dropping a few institutions each year except 1978 when it gained slightly with two new taverns opening.

A pattern of taverns that contributes to the institutional-item scores is worth mentioning. Recall that the point value of a particular tavern received was based on the price of a pint of wine. Tavern owners quite consciously maintain certain prices, quite arbitrarily at that, on pints of wine. They do this because they know that low-priced pints attract "winos." A pattern, with exceptions, was noticed in the process of data collection. In core Skid Row areas, wine prices in taverns were uniformly low. A rough ring of taverns just outside a core Skid Row area would have uniformly high wine prices. Beyong the ring, prices were usually in a middle range. Clearly a containment policy was in force. Ballard, an area identified in exploratory forays as a definite relocation destination for former Skid Row men (among other ways, by a welfare department official who said Ballard was a low-cost-housing area to which displaced Skid Row men were directed), has around twelve liquor-serving establishments in the four-block strip where data were gathered. Every one that sells wine charges the same high price.

Transitory Items

The transitory-item total scores shown in table 4–4 also show a pattern that is essentially one of decline but with almost twice as many increases from

Table 4-4
Transitory-Item Total Scores, by Year and Area, with Percentages of
Yearly Totals and Proportions of 1972 Scores

Area	1972	1973	1974	1975	1976	1977	1978[a]
International	134	148	102	85	103	124	129
District	11.2	11.5	09.8	8.0	11.0	15.4	12.2
	(1)	(1.10)	(0.76)	(0.63)	(0.77)	(0.92)	(0.96)
Pioneer Square area	572	616	504	487	510	309	546
	47.9	48.0	48.2	45.8	54.4	38.3	51.6
	(1)	(1.07)	(0.88)	(0.85)	(0.89)	(0.54)	(0.95)
First Avenue area	117	139	131	143	60	90	63
	9.8	10.8	12.5	13.4	6.4	11.2	6.0
	(1)	(1.19)	(1.12)	(1.22)	(0.51)	(0.77)	(0.54)
Belltown	222	253	187	233	143	213	263
	18.6	19.7	17.9	21.9	15.3	26.4	24.9
	(1)	(1.14)	(0.84)	(1.05)	(0.64)	(0.96)	(1.18)
Pike Street	26	27	30	22	11	0	2
	2.2	2.1	2.9	2.1	1.2	0.0	0.2
	(1)	(1.04)	(1.15)	(0.85)	(0.42)	(0.00)	(0.08)
Fremont	5	5	7	6	10	10	—[b]
	0.4	0.3	0.7	0.6	1.1	1.2	
		(1972 baseline too small for meaningful comparison)					
Ballard	41	31	22	13	13	10	—[b]
	3.4	2.4	2.1	1.2	1.4	1.2	
	(1)	(0.76)	(0.54)	(0.32)	(0.32)	(0.24)	
Tacoma	78	64	62	74	87	51	55
	6.5	5.0	5.9	7.0	9.3	6.3	5.2
	(1)	(0.82)	(0.79)	(1.02)	(1.16)	(0.65)	(0.71)
Totals	1,195	1,283	1,045	1,063	937	807	1,058
	100.0[c]	99.8	100.0	100.0	100.0	100.0	100.0
	(1)	(1.07)	(0.87)	(0.89)	(0.78)	(0.67)	(0.88)

Note: In each group of three numbers, the top number indicates the raw score, the middle indicates percentage, and the bottom indicates proportion of 1972 scores.

[a]The 1978 figures are adjusted to include estimates of scores that uncounted blocks would have contributed.

[b]Fremont and Ballard were not covered at all in 1978.

[c]Totals are not all 100.0 % because of rounding.

one year to the next as registered in the institutional-item-score totals for the eight areas—21 out of a possible 46 as opposed to 11 institutional-item-score yearly increases. Given the inherent variability of the data, few outstanding cells appear in table 4-4. Most striking is the low 1977 score of the Pioneer Square area, but as the count is up the following year, the significance of this exceptional year is dubious. The First Avenue area appears to have sustained a substantial decline after 1975, and the V-shaped pattern of the International District scores over the years is unique.

Most interesting, however, are comparisons that can be made between the transitory-item scores in table 4-4 and the institutional-item scores in table 4-3. The percentages of yearly totals contributed by various areas to institutional-item totals and to transitory-item totals differ widely in some cases. For example, the Pioneer Square area contributes an average of 20.6 percent of institutional-item scores over the years in contrast to 47.7 percent of the transitory-item scores. The corresponding average contributions of Belltown are 27.2 percent to institutional-item scores and 20.7 percent to transitory-item scores. For the First Avenue area, the corresponding average contributions are 16.1 to institutional-item scores and 10 percent to transitory-item scores. The other areas contribute less disproportionately, with Tacoma only slightly less so. Only International District besides the Pioneer Square area has a higher yearly average percentage contribution to transitory items than to institutional items, and the difference is only 0.8 percent. Skid Row activities take place in the Pioneer Square area most, while the institutions that serve Skid Row men are mostly away from the Pioneer Square area. The symbolic, historical position of the Pioneer Square area may well be an important factor that continues to make it *the* Skid Road.

An interesting question can be addressed through a comparison of the institutional- and transitory-item scores. Does a change in transitory-item score follow a change in institutional score, or do institutions follow behaviors? Which is primary? If a change in institutional-item score from one year to the next—a decrease, for example—is followed by a similar change in transitory-item score in the same area a year later, a case of institutional primacy can be said to exist. If such an institutional change is followed by a transitory-item change in the opposite direction, then that is a case of lack of institutional primacy. If a change in transitory-item score is followed by an institutional-item score the following year, then a case of transitory-item primacy exists, and if the transitory-item-score change is followed by an institutional-item-score change in the opposite direction, then a lack of transitory-item primacy exists. For example, the transitory-item count in Belltown in 1972 is 222. It rises to 253 in 1975. The institutional-item score in 1973 in Belltown is 115, and it drops to 108 in 1974. This disconfirms transitory-item primacy. In Tacoma in 1972 the transitory-item count is 78, and it drops to 64 the following year. The institutional-item count drops from 58 to 53 between 1973 and 1974, so this is a case of transitory-item primacy.

Examining all possibilities of such comparisons between table 4-3 and 4-4, one finds that the primacy of institutions is confirmed twenty times and disconfirmed thirteen times. The primacy of transitory items is confirmed seventeen times and disconfirmed sixteen times. (Most cases are confirmed both ways because most of the changes are decreases.) In the case of

no change in score from one year to the next, no confirmation or disconfir-
mation is counted. While simple directional difference is a rough measure
(quantitative measurement could conceivably be applied), the finding that
the balance tips in favor of the primacy of institutions in determining the
location of Skid Row confirms the conclusion of Churchill (1976) that Skid
Row will follow the missions. However, the fact that the Pioneer Square
area maintains its behavioral aspects of Skid Row-ness while losing its institutions is a dominant example to the contrary. Perhaps a plausible generalization is that, barring overriding cultural factors, institutions usually will
determine locations of behavior. These cultural factors are, recall from
chapter 2, the central focus of Firey's (1946; 1947) cultural-ecology hypothesis.

Derelicts. The individual transitory items shown in tables 4-5 through
4-7—derelicts, loiterers, and discarded bottles respectively—together make
up 94.4 percent of the total transitory-item scores on the average over all
seven years. The most obvious pattern in table 4-5—observations of derelicts—is the overall decline in each area. The Pioneer Square area usually
generates at least twice as many observations of derelicts as the next highest
scoring area, Belltown, except in 1977 when only 57 derelicts were observed
in the Pioneer Square area. The decline in number of derelicts in the Pioneer
Square area is less than in any of the other areas except Fremont, which had
so few in the initial years that virtually no decline was possible. Relative to
all other areas, each area usually holds its own, indicating that no shift in
Skid Row-ness, as measured by this item, has taken place. The few exceptionally high years are usually followed by more-average years. Were it not
for a below-average year in 1977, the Pioneer Square area might be said to
be relatively increasing in number of derelicts. Derelicts, at two centrality
points each, over all years account for 49.1 percent of the total points for
transitory items. This average is made up of percentages varying from 64.4
percent in 1972 downward to 30.6 percent in 1978. This decline is much the
same in each area, with the Pioneer Square area showing the least decline
and Belltown and International District showing the most.

Loiterers. The observations of loiterers, shown in table 4-6, generated patterns distinctly different than the observations of derelicts. The overall
loiterer pattern is one of relatively low numbers in 1972 when compared to
1973, 1974, and 1975. Then there is a decrease in 1976 and 1977 and another
increase in 1978. Notable variation from this pattern occurred in Tacoma
and the Pioneer Square area in 1976 when those areas registered proportion-
ately greater numbers of loiterers than in other years. In all years but 1972
and 1975, the Pioneer Square area had about three times the number of
loiterers observed in the two other areas where loiterers were most abun-

Table 4-5
**Observations of Derelicts, by Area and Year, with Percentages of
Yearly Totals and Proportions of 1972 Scores**

Area	1972	1973	1974	1975	1976	1977	1978[a]
International	38	42	27	18	28	10	15
District	9.9	11.4	9.9	7.1	12.1	7.3	9.3
	(1)	(1.11)	(0.71)	(0.47)	(0.74)	(0.26)	(0.39)
Pioneer Square area	171	160	111	119	123	57	100
	44.4	43.5	39.9	47.2	53.0	41.6	61.7
	(1)	(0.94)	(0.65)	(0.70)	(0.72)	(0.33)	(0.58)
First Avenue area	39	44	45	34	19	17	11
	10.1	12.0	16.2	13.5	8.2	12.4	6.8
	(1)	(1.13)	(1.15)	(0.87)	(0.49)	(0.44)	(0.28)
Belltown	82	80	60	55	33	40	25
	21.3	21.8	21.6	21.8	14.2	29.2	15.4
	(1)	(0.98)	(0.73)	(0.67)	(0.40)	(0.49)	(0.30)
Pike Street	10	8	5	3	4	0	1
	2.6	2.2	1.8	1.2	1.7	0.0	0.6
	(1)	(0.80)	(0.50)	(0.30)	(0.40)	(0.00)	(0.10)
Fremont	1	2	3	2	2	1	
	0.3	0.5	1.1	0.8	0.9	0.7	—[b]
			(1972 baseline too small for meaningful comparison)				
Ballard	13	12	7	2	5	3	
	3.4	3.3	2.5	0.8	2.2	2.2	—[b]
	(1)	(0.92)	(0.54)	(0.15)	(0.38)	(0.23)	
Tacoma	31	20	20	19	18	9	10
	8.1	5.4	7.2	7.5	7.8	6.6	6.1
	(1)	(0.65)	(0.65)	(0.61)	(0.58)	(0.29)	(0.32)
Totals	385	368	278	252	232	137	162
	100.1[c]	100.1	99.9	99.9	100.1	100.0	99.9
	(1)	(0.96)	(0.72)	(0.65)	(0.60)	(0.36)	(0.42)

Note: In each group of three numbers, the top number indicates the raw score, the middle indicates percentage, and the bottom indicates proportion of 1972 scores.
[a]The 1978 figures are adjusted to include estimates of scores that uncounted blocks would have contributed.
[b]Fremont and Ballard were not covered at all in 1978.
[c]Totals are not all 100.0 % because of rounding.

dant—International District and the First Avenue area. In 1972 and 1975, the ratio was just 3 to 1. This is largely because of Occidental Square, the spot contributing by far the most to the yearly count of loiterers, also the one large and two small parks near city hall, and Pioneer Square itself. International District, the First Avenue area, and Belltown had roughly similar numbers of loiterers each year, with some variation. As with derelicts, no clear trend of movement from one area to another over the years is evident. Loiterers, at one centrality point each, make up 33.8 per-

Table 4-6
Observations of Loiterers, by Area and Year, with Percentages of
Yearly Totals and Proportions of 1972 Scores

Area	1972	1973	1974	1975	1976	1977	1978[a]
International	47	52	42	33	30	52	74
District	16.3	13.4	11.1	8.2	9.1	17.3	18.1
	(1)	(1.11)	(0.89)	(0.70)	(0.64)	(1.11)	(1.57)
Pioneer Square area	140	215	198	194	202	129	230
	48.6	55.3	52.4	48.4	61.0	43.0	56.2
	(1)	(1.53)	(1.41)	(1.39)	(1.44)	(0.92)	(1.64)
First Avenue area	29	34	37	67	17	46	35
	10.1	8.7	9.8	16.7	5.1	15.3	8.6
	(1)	(1.17)	(1.28)	(2.31)	(0.59)	(1.58)	(1.21)
Belltown	41	54	55	63	30	48	53
	14.2	13.9	14.6	15.7	9.1	16.0	13.0
	(1)	(1.32)	(1.34)	(1.54)	(0.73)	(1.17)	(1.29)
Pike Street	6	8	19	12	2	0	0
	2.1	2.1	5.0	3.0	0.6	0.0	0.0
	(1972 baseline too small for meaningful comparison)						
Fremont	3	1	1	2	4	3	
	1.0	0.3	0.3	0.5	1.2	1.0	—[b]
	(1972 baseline too small for meaningful comparison)						
Ballard	9	4	4	1	0	3	—[b]
	(1972 baseline too small for meaningful comparison)						
Tacoma	13	21	22	29	46	19	17
	4.5	5.4	5.8	7.2	13.9	6.3	4.2
	(1)	(1.62)	(1.69)	(2.23)	(3.54)	(1.46)	(1.31)
Totals	288	389	378	401	331	300	409
	99.9[c]	100.1	100.1	99.9	100.0	99.9	100.1
	(1)	(1.35)	(1.34)	(1.39)	(1.15)	(1.04)	(1.42)

Note: In each group of three numbers, the top number indicates the raw score, the middle indicates percentage, and the bottom indicates proportion of 1972 scores.

[a]The 1978 figures are adjusted to include estimates of scores that uncounted blocks would have contributed.

[b]Fremont and Ballard were not covered at all in 1978.

[c]Totals are not all 100.0 % because of rounding.

cent of the overall number of transitory-item points, making up much less than average in 1972, 24.1 percent. Loiterers make up only around 20 percent of the transitory-item count in Belltown except in 1974 (42 percent) and 1973 (27 percent). Counts of loiterers make up around 40 percent of the total transitory-item count in the Pioneer Square area except in 1972 (24.5 percent) and 1973 (34.9 percent). In International District the percentages over the years are more variable, but overall they are higher. Tacoma's are variable and lower.

Table 4-7
Observations of Discarded Bottles, by Area and Year, with Percentages of Yearly Totals and Proportions of 1972 Scores

Area	1972	1973	1974	1975	1976	1977	1978[a]
International	8	12	6	7	7	14	22
District	7.3	7.6	7.1	8.0	10.3	10.2	10.4
	(1)	(1.50)	(0.75)	(0.88)	(0.88)	(1.75)	(2.75)
Pioneer Square area	75	48	54	19	13	39	53
	68.2	30.4	72.0	21.8	19.1	28.5	25.1
	(1)	(0.64)	(0.72)	(0.25)	(0.17)	(0.52)	(0.71)
First Avenue area	10	65	4	8	2	10	5
	9.1	41.1	5.3	9.2	2.9	7.3	2.4
	(1)	(6.50)	(0.40)	(0.80)	(0.20)	(1.00)	(0.50)
Belltown	11	33	9	38	37	60	116
	10.0	20.9	12.0	43.7	54.4	43.8	55.0
	(1)	(3.00)	(0.82)	(3.45)	(3.36)	(5.45)	(10.55)
Pike Street	0	0	1	4	1	0	0
	0.0	0.0	1.3	4.6	1.5	0.0	0.0
			(1972 baseline too small for meaningful comparison)				
Fremont	0	0	0	0	2	5	
	0.0	0.0	0.0	0.0	2.9	3.6	b
			(1972 baseline too small for meaningful comparison)				
Ballard	3	0	1	6	3	1	
	2.7	0.0	1.3	6.9	4.4	0.7	—b
			(1972 baseline too small for meaningful comparison)				
Tacoma	3	0	0	5	3	8	15
	2.7	0.0	0.0	5.7	4.4	5.8	7.1
			(1972 baseline too small for meaningful comparison)				
Totals	110	158	75	87	68	137	211
	100.0c	100.0	99.9	99.9	99.9	99.9	100.0
	(1)	(1.44)	(0.68)	(0.79)	(0.62)	(1.25)	(1.92)

Note: In each group of three numbers, the top number indicates the raw score, the middle indicates percentage, and the bottom indicates proportion of 1972 scores.
[a]The 1978 figures are adjusted to include estimates of scores that uncounted blocks would have contributed.
[b]Fremont and Ballard were not covered at all in 1978.
[c]Totals are not all 100.0 % because of rounding.

Discarded Bottles. The overall pattern of observations of discarded bottles shown in table 4-7 is one of essentially high early-year counts and high later-year counts with a dip in 1974, 1975, and 1976. The exceptions to this area are a high percentage in the Pioneer Square area in 1974, a low percentage in Belltown in 1972, and low early years in Tacoma. A relative change that is apparent is a rise in the percentage of bottles observed in Belltown. The change from an average relative percentage of 14.3 percent in the first three years to an average of 49.2 percent in the last four years is one of the more-dramatic trends observable in these tables. Belltown surpasses the Pioneer Square area in observations of discarded bottles in 1975 and remains substantially ahead through 1978. The discussion of discarded bottles in appendix A casts some doubt on the validity of the conclusion that this one aspect of Skid Row is changing locations, but the data clearly indicate a change. The Belltown count of 116 discarded bottles in 1976 when the next highest year registered 60 is in part due to the exceptional find of 27 bottles in one doorway on First Avenue. Unbroken discarded bottles, at one cen-trality point each, make up 11.5 percent of the total transitory-item count. Belltown in the later years is the single important deviation from this average. The counts of bottles elsewhere each year make up less than or about the same percentage of the total transitory-item count for each area.

Recumbant Loiterers and Bottle Gangs. Recumbant loiterers and bottle gangs were observed so infrequently they do not merit a table. Briefly, in all seven years of the study there were 3 recumbant loiterers in International District, 68 in the Pioneer Square area, 1 in the First Avenue area, 24 in Belltown, 5 in Tacoma, 1 in Ballard, and none in Fremont or on Pike Street. Perhaps significantly, 17 of the 24 observed in Belltown were observed in 1977 and 1978. This corresponds to the sharp increase in observed discarded bottles in Belltown in the last years of the study. It could be that heavy drinkers are tending more to frequent Belltown. However, the Pioneer Square area shows no decrease in number of recumbant loiterers in 1977 and 1978.

Given the increase in number of recumbant loiterers and discarded bottles, one might expect an increase in number of bottle gangs observed in Belltown in the later years as well. This did not happen, however. Of a total of 14 gangs observed in Belltown in seven years, only 5 were observed in the last three years, but bottle gangs are observed so infrequently compared to their obvious presence—namely, discarded bottles—(solitary drinkers are seldom seen either) that the fact that only 5 were seen in the last three years only fails to confirm the shift of drinkers to Belltown. It does not disconfirm it either. Elsewhere over the seven-year observation period, 7 bottle gangs were observed in International District, 34 in the Pioneer Square area, one in the First Avenue area, 1 on Pike Street, 2 in Tacoma, 3 in Ballard, and none in Fremont. In the Pioneer Square area, the exceptional year was 1978 with 8 bottlegangs, and the second high year was 1975 with 5.

Special-Category Blocks

Measurement of the relative movement of Skid Row is shown in table 4–8 in a way independent of the geographical-area divisions used in tables 4–2

Table 4–8

Grand-Total Skid Row-ness Scores of Special-Category Blocks, by Year, with Percentages of Yearly Totals and Proportions of 1972 Scores

Special Categories	1972	1973	1974	1975	1976	1977	1978[a]
Periphery	145	159	105	148	14	173	133
blocks	9.0	9.4	7.3	10.7	8.4	14.9	10.1
	(1)	(1.10)	(0.72)	(1.02)	(0.72)	(1.19)	(0.92)
Park blocks	253	400	282	383	396	218	497
	15.7	23.7	19.7	27.7	32.0	18.8	37.8
	(1)	(1.58)	(1.11)	(1.51)	(1.57)	(0.86)	(1.96)
High-count blocks	114	77	87	41	48	58	36
	7.1	4.6	6.1	3.0	3.9	5.0	2.7
	(1)	(0.68)	(0.76)	(0.36)	(0.42)	(0.51)	(0.32)
All other blocks	1,101	1,050	959	812	690	710	648
	68.3	62.3	66.9	58.7	55.7	61.3	49.3
	(1)	(0.95)	(0.87)	(0.83)	(0.63)	(0.64)	(0.59)
Totals	1,613	1,686	1,433	1,384	1,238	1,159	1,314
	100.1[b]	100.0	100.0	100.0	100.0	100.0	99.9
	(1)	(1.05)	(0.89)	(0.86)	(0.77)	(0.72)	(0.81)

Note: In each group of three numbers, the top number indicates the raw score, the middle indicates percentage, and the bottom indicates proportion of 1972 scores.

[a]The 1978 figures are adjusted to include estimates of scores that uncounted blocks would have contributed.

[b]Totals are not all 100.0 % because of rounding.

through 4–7. Blocks in all of the Seattle downtown areas were grouped into four categories: (1) Blocks that included counts taken in a park or public square, fourteen in all; (2) blocks generating high counts and not bordering a park or square, four in all; (3) blocks on the periphery of International District, the Pioneer Square area, the First Avenue area, and Belltown, forty-two blocks in all; and (4) all 129 other blocks. The pattern of overall decline in Skid Row–ness is reversed in the park blocks in large part because some parks were created and expanded during the course of the study, while renovation elsewhere made Skid Row characteristics less in character with the surroundings. The periphery blocks also fail to reflect the decline pattern, showing instead ups and downs, but they usually register a nondeclining pattern. The high-count blocks away from parks show the most drastic proportion of loss of Skid Row-ness count of any category of blocks, special or geographic area. Significant numbers of Skid Row men and their institutions are no longer present on formerly core turf.

Summary

In summary, the street data show that Skid Row has been declining in the 1970s in Seattle. No new Skid Row area is opening up, not in outlying areas of Seattle, not in another area adjacent to the CBD, and in Tacoma no spillover is apparent during the time of decline in Seattle. In fact, a corresponding decline has occurred in Tacoma. Certain years—namely, 1973 and 1978—register sizable increases over the previous years, indicating that Skid Row is still quite capable of fluctuating. This fact is accentuated by the selection of August as data-collection month. August probably marks the nadir of the Skid Row-population curve. In winter the fluctuations of the economy would be most evident on Skid Row. Two noteworthy variations from the pattern of decline are, first, the fairly strong pattern of maintenance of the transient characteristics of Skid Row in the face of the decline of Skid Row institutions observed in the Pioneer Square area and, second, the apparent increase in open-air drinking and its aftermath in the Belltown area.

Police Data

As indicated in chapter 3, Seattle Police Department data were used in two ways to discover trends in Skid Row-location changes. First, aggregate figures on arrests for typical Skid Row offenses by year and census tract were thought likely to show increases and decreases that would correspond to increases and decreases in Skid Row population and activities. Second, a four-year record of the locations of arrests of certain persons was examined. These persons were arrested in the first year, 1973, in a Skid Row-area census tract on a charge typical of Skid Row arrest. Concentrations of subsequent arrests were thought likely to suggest places to which displaced Skid Row men go.

   In Seattle, during the years for which data were available, 1973 through 1976, crimes typical of Skid Row were unlawful disposition of liquor, which includes public drunkenness; possession of an open bottle in public, as well as manufacturing alcohol without a license; selling or giving alcohol to a minor; disturbing the peace, which includes obstructing traffic, disrupting an assembly, and various types of noisy public behavior; begging, which is asking for money or food in public but which does not cover street musicians; loitering, which usually amounts to being present in or near some place of business such as a hotel or restaurant when the proprietor wants you to leave; and urinating in public. In October 1976, these offenses were reclassified, and more-specific charges have been used since then.

Aggregate Arrest Data

Arrests for these offenses are shown by year and census tract in table 4-9. Also shown are the proportions of such arrests occurring in the winter

Table 4–9
Arrests for Typical Skid Row Offenses, by Year and Census Tract

Census tract[a]	Number of Arrests, Percentage of Total, Winter Proportion			
	1973	1974	1975	1976
Belltown	803	175	62	62
	6.4%	1.5%	3.2%	2.7%
	(0.24)	(0.40)	(0.15)	(0.10)
First Avenue area and part of the CBD	3,959	1,256	446	665
	31.5%	10.6%	22.9%	28.8%
	(0.24)	(0.24)	(0.14)	(0.13)
CBD	591	225	92	76
	4.7%	1.9%	4.7%	3.3%
	(0.23)	(0.39)	(0.23)	(0.26)
Upper Pike, just northeast of the CBD	163	32	11	4
	1.3%	0.3%	0.6%	0.2%
	(0.26)	(0.53)	(0.18)	(0.25)
Northeast of the Upper Pike area	251	62	11	21
	2.0%	0.5%	0.6%	0.9%
	(0.24)	(0.31)	(0.27)	(0.33)
Southeast of the CBD	219	59	25	14
	1.7%	0.5%	1.3%	0.6%
	(0.24)	(0.37)	(0.40)	(0.14)
Pioneer Square area	1,214	375	276	480
	9.7%	3.2%	14.2%	20.8%
	(0.28)	(0.16)	(0.05)	(0.08)
International District	376	55	23	24
	3.0%	0.5%	1.2%	1.0%
	(0.29)	(0.29)	(0.09)	(0.00)
Subtotal	7,576	2,239	946	1,346
	60.3%	19.0%	48.7%	58.3%
	(0.25)	(0.27)	(0.13)	(0.12)
All other Seattle census tracts	4,990	9,598	1,000	962
	39.7%	81.0%	51.3%	41.7%
	(0.23)	(0.14)	(0.18)	(0.12)
Total	12,556	11,837	1,946	2.308
	100.0%	100.0%	100.0%	100.0%
	(0.24)	(0.16)	(0.16)	(0.12)

[a]Appendix B shows the numberic designations of the Seattle Police Department census tracts (Seattle Police Department 1975; 1974; 1973). Also shown are the corresponding U.S. Census Bureau numeric designations. The areas are identical. The common names used are more descriptive of the areas than census or police numbers would be for the average or informed reader. The areas' correspondence between common name and official designation is rough, but not so rough as to mislead.

months of December, January, and February. Skid Row is a winter haven
for transient and seasonal workers, and particular census tracts might well
accommodate more of these winter residents than others. Winter-arrest
records could conceivably show changes over time in wintering-area
preference.

As Blumberg, Shipley, and Barsky (1978) discovered in Philadelphia,
Skid Row–arrest records show more than Skid Row–crime rates. Table 4–9
shows drastic changes between 1973 and 1974, even more drastic than the
changes between 1974 and 1975, the year that marks the decriminalization
of public intoxication in the state of Washington. In 1973, the Skid Row
and adjacent census tracts, including the CBD, registered 60 percent of the
12,556 total arrests for typical Skid Row offenses. In 1974, with 11,837 such
arrests, Skid Row and adjacent tracts registered only 19 percent of the city's
total. This represents an absolute decline of 70.4 percent in arrests for
typical Skid Row offenses, from 7,576 to 2,239, in and around the CBD,
and an absolute increase of 92.3 percent, from 4,990 to 9,598, in the outlying areas of the city. One might infer a rational policy from this change in
enforcement pattern. Could this pattern represent an attempt to apply less-
than-subtle pressure to drive offenders into Skid Row and adjacent areas so
that the following year the new civilian Detox program could net them in?

Perhaps, however, a more-political motive was behind the enforcement
change. Arresting fewer persons for typical Skid Row offenses in and
around Skid Row and the CBD could make Skid Row–ness more visible and
thus make the Detox program seem more necessary and appreciated,
perhaps mollifying public outcry over the expense of the Detox program.
Also, the sharp rise in arrests for Skid Row–type offenses away from Skid
Row and the CBD might cause higher-status offenders to come to appreciate Detox as an alternative to embarrasing police contact. In fact, at this
time, budget cutbacks in the police department reduced the number of
officers on the beat in the downtown area, and more police work involved
responding to calls.

The gross changes in the pattern of arrests shown in table 4–9 make
variation between Skid Row–area census tracts questionable as indicators of
changing Skid Row location. However, problematic, the changes evident in
the percentages of total arrests for typical Skid Row offenses are, in addition to the remarkable changes between 1973 and 1974, a relatively large
and growing percentage of arrests in the Pioneer Square area in 1975 and
1976 and a return to a high percentage of arrests in the First Avenue area in
1976.

The value, for the detection of Skid Row shifts, of variation in proportions of arrests occurring in winter months is similarly problematic, chiefly
because of the overall changes concurrent with the creation of Detox. The
winter proportions, the third figure in each cell of table 4–9, vary markedly

after 1973. In 1973, in census tracts around the CBD and in the rest of the city, winter proportions of arrests are approximately what would be expected by chance—that is, around one-fourth of the total number of arrests. This could mean that winter migration into Seattle's Skid Row areas is minimal. It could also mean that, since cold-weather confinement reduces risk of arrest, the effect immigration in winter might have on arrest rates is canceled. In 1974, the year before Detox took over the job of removing drunken people from the street and the year the police systematically began phasing out of that job, the numbers of arrests are so much lower than the previous year's numbers that fluctuations in the winter proportions of arrests may not have clear meaning. However, in 1974 in the CBD, Belltown, and the census tracts northeast and southeast of the CBD, the proportions of winter arrests for Skid Row–type offenses are substantially up from the previous year. This probably indicates that police in 1974 tended to ignore Skid Row–type offenses except in winter when Skid Row offenders are often in dire need of shelter. The very low proportion of winter pickups in the Pioneer Square area in 1974 is probably due not to police's ignoring the plight of people in need of shelter but to the city's contracting with the missions to provide bed and board to needy people, a practice periodically found to be expedient. After 1974, the activities of the Detox patrol probably account for the lower proportions of arrests in wintertime for typical Skid Row offenses in the Skid Row areas. The Pioneer Square area, International District, Belltown, and the First Avenue area each shows large decreases in the proportion of winter arrests after Detox began operating. Corresponding decreases are not evident in other census tracts. Even after the creation of Detox, the police are often the first contact (if only visual) public inebriates have with official inebriate management. Police call in to Detox to alert them to probable pickups. Perhaps police and others attribute only drunkenness to public inebriates in Skid Row and downtown areas, whereas when a public inebriate is spotted elsewhere, police action ensues.

Compounding the problems of inference from police data is the fact that police discretion is clearly evident in the variation in charge preferred in the process of removing Skid Row persons from the street. Table 4–10 shows the variation among typical Skid Row charges between 1973 and 1976. The offense of urinating in public shows a sharp change in enforcement between 1974 and 1975, with no charges at all prior to 1975. To this author's knowledge, no public toilets were open in 1973 and 1974 that were closed afterwards. Also, for some reason, not a single person was charged with the offense of begging in 1975, and no person was charged with loitering in 1976, but both categories of offense were used in all other years.

Overall, the aggregate arrest data clearly show more about the relations of the people to Skid Row than about Skid Row itself. The dramatic

Table 4-10
Number of Charges Preferred in Typical Skid Row-Area Arrests and Their Respective Percentages of All Arrests in Seattle, by Year

Charge	1973	1974	1975	1976
Unlawful disposition of liquor	11,213	10,117	941	1,534
	30.4%	28.0%	3.6%	5.5%
Disturbing the peace	882	1,000	619	365
	2.4%	2.8%	2.4%	1.3%
Begging	194	364	0	154
	0.5%	1.0%	0.0%	0.5%
Loitering	277	356	175	0
	0.8, ·	1.0%	0.7%	0.0%
Urinating in public	0	0	211	255
	0.0%	0.0%	0.8%	0.9%
Subtotal	12,566	11,834	1,946	2,308
	34.1%	32.6%	7.5%	8.2%
All other charges	24,221	24,323	24,102	25,764
	65.8%	67.3%	92.5%	91.8%
Total	36,787	36,163	26,048	28,072
	99.9%[a]	99.9%	100.0%	100.0%

[a]Totals are not all 100.0% because of rounding.

changes in arrest figures almost certainly do not reflect similar changes in presence of Skid Row characteristics. However, the data set is not totally bereft of relevant meaning. After Detox took over management of public inebriates, police activity on Skid Row decreased, but it decreased least in the Pioneer Square area. This is consistent with street observations indicating that the Pioneer Square area maintained many of its Skid Row characteristics, chiefly the behavioral indicators (transitory items) of Skid Row-ness. The area with the highest level of Skid Row-offense arrests, before and after the creation of the Detox program, is the police district that includes the First Avenue area and part of the CBD. Very heavy foot traffic and the concentrated commercial nature of this area probably warrant more patrolling and make police less conducive to toleration of Skid Row men's behavior. While the aggregate police data do not offer many answers, the same data, when arranged in the form of individual "rap sheets," provide some specific answers.

Individual Records

The arrest records of 250 randomly drawn persons were examined. The population from which these records were drawn consisted of all persons who were arrested in 1973 for a typical Skid Row offense in any one of four

Skid Row census tracts. 1973 was the first year such records were available. Locations of subsequent arrests of these 250 selected arrestees show, to a degree, shifts in Skid Row-ness, at least short-term movement if not migration. In addition to arrestees' first bookings in 1973, 501 subsequent bookings were recorded in the years 1973 through 1976. Of these 501 repeat arrests, 18 (36.1 percent) occurred in the same four census tracts that delimited the population. Another 35 repeat arrests (7 percent) occurred in census tracts immediately adjacent to the four Skid Row tracts. The census tract southeast of the CBD, north of and adjacent to Yesler Way, was the tract where most of these 35 arrests occurred. Ten other census tracts each accounted for more than five repeat offenses. These census tracts encompass the University of Washington, Salmon Bay Fisherman's Terminal (a bridge length away from Ballard), the area adjacent to the Seattle Center and Space Needle (immediately northwest of the CBD), two census tracts in the First Hill area (just northeast of the CBD), three census tracts adjacent to Yesler Way and within one mile of the CBD, the census tract including the Veterans Hospital and a large park, and the Northgate-area census tract, which includes the city bus parking area and which is six miles from the CBD. The Northgate census tract has the highest crime rate of any area in Seattle away from the CBD (Seattle Police Department 1973; 1974; 1975).

In the downtown census tracts, there was no apparent pattern of persons' being arrested first in one particular tract and subsequently in another. Of the 181 Skid Row-area arrests subsequent to the first arrest, in the downtown tracts, 45 percent occurred in the same census tract as the first offense. Changes in arrest location from one area to another appear approximately as frequently as shifts in the opposite direction.

While a directional shift within the Skid Row tracts is not evident, another sort of movement is. The "rap sheets" show home address, and of the 431 bookings for offenses taking place in the four Skid Row census tracts, only 55 (12.8 percent) involved arrests of people who lived in the census tract of the arrest. Another 35.3 percent lived in one of the Skid Row census tracts other than the one in which the arrest took place. More than half of the Skid Row-area arrests involved people who did not live there. While the residential nature of Skid Row has diminished, the sociocultural nature of the area continues to be manifest. However, while Skid Row is still a homing ground for Skid Row behavior, it is also true that the area does not hold people as it once did. The insiders and the outsiders apparently have more freedom now in crossing what boundary is left of the Skid Row of old.

Medical Examiner's Records

A source of data suggested by the disaffiliated nature of the population under study is the records of addresses of deceased persons who had no known relative and whose funeral was paid for by the county or an institution such as the Mariner's Union or the St. Vincent DePaul Society. The King County Medical Examiner Division of the Seattle-King County Department of Health is responsible for investigating deaths of any sort other than those attended by a physician in a normal medical setting. Specifically, deaths that come under the jurisdiction of the medical examiner are defined by statute and include all violent deaths and deaths resulting from crime, deaths that came suddenly to one in apparent good health, deaths occurring under suspicious circumstances, deaths due to a violent contagious disease, deaths occurring in jail or prison, deaths due to premature or stillbirth, and most relevant to Skid Row, deaths in which the body is unclaimed by relatives or friends (King County Medical Examiner 1976). In table 4-11, the addresses of persons who died with no relatives identifying themselves as such are listed by area. Data were collected in 1972 to locate emergent Skid Row areas and were subsequently not collected until 1978 when their longitudinal-comparison value was realized. In 1978, only the past one year's records were readily available.

While absolute numbers of unclaimed bodies are down in 1978 as compared with 1972, viewing either absolute numbers or relative percentages makes it clear that Belltown experienced the greatest growth in unclaimed bodies. The only other area showing a notable increase is the area from one to two miles from the CBD. The geographic center of this area in relation to unclaimed bodies is the Broadway business district, northeast of the CBD. Casual observation in 1978 recorded other Skid Row characteristics there as well. The area registering the greatest decrease in the number of unclaimed bodies, and the largest percentage drop, is the Pioneer Square area. The diminshed residential nature of the Pioneer Square area certainly accounts for this drop. Decreases in the number of unclaimed bodies also occurred in International District, the CBD, near Pike Street, and within six blocks of CDB. In summary, these findings indicate a decrease in (mostly older) disaffiliated people living in and around the CBD except in Belltown.

Census Data

The understanding of Seattle's Skid Row areas to be gained from decennial census statistics from 1950 through 1970 (U.S. Bureau of the Census 1952; 1962; 1972) is in the demographic documentation of the character of the area as a haven of disaffiliated persons. Five variables reported in census-tract summaries provide data useful in determining long-term changes in Skid Row-ness:

1. Sex ratio, or number of men per 100 women;
2. Median number of people per household;

Table 4–11
Areas of Home Address of People Who Died in Seattle between 1 July 1971
and 30 June 1972 and between 1 July 1977 and 30 June 1978, with No
Known Living Relatives

	1971–1972		1977–1978	
Home Area	November	Percentage	November	Percentage
Belltown (within three blocks of street-observation-data area, not including the CBD)	14	14.3	20	25.3
First Avenue area	3	3.1	4	5.1
Third-Sixth Avenue, CBD, (Stewart-James)	12	12.2	6	7.6
Upper Pike (within three blocks of Pike, 6th-8th but not including the CBD)	9	9.2	4	5.1
Pioneer Square area	21	21.4	13	16.4
International District	12	12.2	6	7.6
Within six blocks of the CBD, not including preceding areas	10	10.2	4	5.1
From six blocks to one mile from the CBD	2	2.0	1	1.3
From one to two miles from the CBD	6	6.1	11	13.9
Beyond two miles from the CBD	9	9.2	10	12.7
Totals	98	99.9[a]	79	100.0

Note: In a small number of cases in the 1971–1972, and in four cases in the 1977–1978 data, no address, not even a transient hotel or mission, was given. In these cases, the address of the death is recorded. The areas shown correspond to the areas utilized for the street observations rather than to census tracts, with additional areas having specified boundaries. The source of these data is the set of case files of the King County Medical Examiner.

[a]Percentage does not total 100.0 because of rounding.

3. Percentage of renter-occupied housing;
4. Percentage of Seattle median rent;
5. Percentage of men over age 14 not in the labor force.

Table 4–12 presents these variables by year for ten Seattle census tracts, tracts that include Skid Row areas and other areas of interest. Appendix C contains a set of specific citations to tables and page numbers in the census bureau's census-tract publications (U.S. Bureau of the Census 1952; 1962; 1972).

The relative Skid Row–ness of an area can be roughly measured using these indicators. In general, and not without exception, based on the literature of Skid Row and on observation indicators, associated with Skid

Row-ness are higher sex ratios, a lower median number of people per household, a higher percentage of rental housing, a lower proportion of median rent, and a higher percentage of men over age 14 not in the labor force. Comparison of the sex ratios of the same census tract between decades as well as comparison between census tracts shows dramatic differences in social surroundings. Sex-ratio extremes in the ten census tracts shown in table 4-12 are 789 (the Pioneer Square-area census tract in 1960) and 66 (the census tract northeast of Upper Pike in 1970). The median number of people per household usually decreases as an area becomes more Skid Row-like because single-person occupancy is characteristic of Skid Row. However, a low number of people per household is not exclusive to Skid Row nor is percentage of renter-occupied dwellings, but both are characteristic of Skid Row, and changes in either could indicate an increase in Skid Row-ness. The percentage of renter-occupied housing units tends to be uniformly high in Skid Row census tracts, with rising percentages from 1950 to 1970 in nearby census tracts. The percentage of Seattle median rent seems a good indication of a neighborhood's relative status in the city. Long-time-Skid Row census tracts are near the bottom of the rent scale. Last, percentage of men aged 14 or over not in the labor force is partially a measurement of Skid Row-ness. This category includes men primarily engaged in doing housework or work at home, seasonal workers during the off-season, retired people unable to work, people not reporting on their employment status, and inmates of institutions. In 1970, men not in the labor force for all of Seattle were categorized as follows: inmates of institutions—1,531; enrolled in school—14,933; others under 65 years old—11,494; others 65 years and older—19,624; total—47,582. Increases in this category in a census tract could well be related to increased Skid Row-ness, especially if they occur with any other indicators. An irregularity with this indicator is that in 1970 the census bureau began reporting the number of 16-year-old or older men (rather than 14 or older as previously) not in the labor force. This irregularity does not greatly affect our interpretation of the figures in table 4-12 because 1970 percentages of men not in the labor force are up rather than down in most of the ten census tracts covered. The change from the 14-or-over age category to the 16-or-over age category cuts out students who would cause numbers to be up. Therefore, increases in 1970 in percentages of men not in the work force can be interpreted as larger than they appear.

Another irregularity exists because of changes in census-tract borders. Three of the ten areas appearing in table 4-12 were not the same in 1970 as they had been in 1960 and 1950. Comparisons between 1970 and earlier figures in these three areas must be viewed as not definitive. In 1950 and 1960, Ballard included a part of another census tract that it did not include in 1970, so decreases in population and number of occupied dwellings may be expected there. The census tract south of Pioneer Square and the

Georgetown tract together are the same in 1970 as they were separately in 1960 and 1950, but Georgetown lost a piece in 1970, and the tract south of Pioneer Square gained it.

In addition to the five variables related directly to Skid Row-ness, table 4-12 includes the population of and number of occupied housing units in each of the ten census tracts covered. The following discussion refers to figures in table 4-12 row by row, area by area, in order roughly from north to south, beginning with Ballard at the top of the table.

Ballard, three miles northwest of the CBD on the waterfront, a Norwegian ethnic community to an extent, appears to have moved only slightly toward Skid Row-like characteristics between 1950 and 1970. Similarly, Fremont, two miles north of the CBD, a noted "hippy" hangout in the late 1960s, maintains non-Skid Row-like characteristics. For both Ballard and Fremont, sex ratios over the years have not been much different from overall Seattle sex ratios. For both, median numbers per household are also like those of the entire city but with more single-person households in 1970. Ballard and Fremont both have somewhat higher percentages of renters than the city as a whole, and their percentages are growing faster than the city's. Rents are close to the median rent of the city and are not dropping relative to other areas. The percentages of men over age 14 not in the labor force in both areas are steady and close to that of the city as a whole, though relatively higher in 1970. Ballard and Fremont are thus two rather average neighborhoods. Measurement at the ends of the last three decades shows in each census tract only a slight tendency toward increased Skid Row-ness.

Belltown, at the northwest end of the CBD, shows both stable and increasing Skid Row characteristics. Sex ratios in this census tract were higher in 1950 and 1960 than in 1970, but in each of the three decades the sex ratio was not less than twice as high as that of the whole city. The consistently low median number of people per household indicates a high proportion of single-occupant dwellings. Renter-occupancy rates in Belltown are among the highest in the city. Along with these characteristics, low and dropping rents and the sharply rising proportion of men not in the labor force identify Belltown as substantially gaining in Skid Row characteristics from 1950 to 1970.

The corridor of First Avenue and nearby blocks, from Belltown to Pioneer Square between the CDB and the waterfront, shows a historical and continuing pattern of occupancy primarily by single men. For example, we find more than five men for every woman living downtown near the waterfront. The percentage of renter-occupied dwellings along First Avenue dropped sharply in 1960 ony to rise to its 1950 level again in 1979. A similar drop in this percentage occurred in Belltown. A slight drop was recorded for the city. Perhaps closings and demolitions in the 1950s focused mostly on rental units, and by 1970 owner-occupants of the area had moved out. More difficult to puzzle out is the extremely small number of occupied housing

Table 4-12
Demographic Data Pertinent to Skid Row-ness, by Area and Year

Area[a]	Year	Sex Ratio[b]	Median Number per Household	Number of Occupied Housing Units	Percentage Renter Occupied	Percentage of Seattle Median Rent[c]	Percentage of Men Aged 14 or over Not in Labor Force[d]	Population
Ballard	1950	107	2.3	2,155	50	92	20	5,823
	1960	97	2.0	2,473	55	88	28	5,220
	1970	91	1.7	2,345	63	91	28	4,428
Fremont	1950	91	2.3	1,914	45	108	19	5,074
	1960	86	2.0	2,282	51	112	25	5,091
	1970	84	1.8	2,708	63	107	27	5,261
Belltown	1950	225	1.2	1,720	90	74	30	3,208
	1960	263	1.1	2,411	77	67	44	2,267
	1970	184	1.1	1,639	88	58	51	2,051
First Avenue area and part of the CDB	1950	495	1.2	277	82	72	46	5,189
	1960	581	1.0	3,940	64	61	54	3,737
	1970	543	1.0	1,313	84	58	62	1,821
CBD	1950	101	1.4	2,470	89	121	26	5,615
	1960	98	1.1	3,309	82	91	32	3,718
	1970	78	1.1	1,985	87	83	34	2,228
Upper Pike just northeast of the CBD	1950	68	1.5	2,267	95	121	21	4,615
	1960	70	1.2	3,398	83	105	24	3,949
	1970	66	1.2	2,766	80	92	40	3,424

Area	Year							
International District	1950	352	1.4	1,348	91	59	51	4,811
	1960	310	1.1	2,369	90	44	48	3,416
	1970	236	1.2	809	96	44	61	1,690
Pioneer Square area	1950	786	1.2	666	88	67	43	3,551
	1960	789	1.1	1,661	95	47	39	2,286
	1970	745	1.0	554	94	42	42	921
South of Pioneer Square	1950	193	2.2	1,300	44	62	24	4,339
	1960	139	1.9	655	56	114	28	1,494
	1970	123	1.9	1,249	46	64	25	2,821
Georgetown	1950	194	2.8	2,512	61	85	23	7,637
	1960	95	2.1	1,425	48	80	21	4,759
	1970	109	1.9	1,098	53	71	22	2,153
All of Seattle	1950	100	2.4	160,872	42	100[c]	22	467,591
	1960	96	2.3	215,981	40	100	22	557,087
	1970	92	2.1	221,973	43	100	25	530,831

[a] Areas include the entire U.S. census tract containing the portion relevant to Skid Row–ness.

[b] Sex ratio is number of men per 100 women.

[c] Seattle median rent in 1950 was $39; in 1960, $66; and in 1970, $106.

[d] In 1970, labor-force characteristics were reported for men aged 16 and over rather than 14 and over as reported in 1960 and 1950.

units in the First Avenue–area census tract in 1950. With the population as it was in 1950 along First Avenue, and with the number of housing units so low, it is surprising that the median number per household is only 1.2. Perhaps a 1949 earthquake that damaged many buildings in that part of Seattle caused people to leave their dwelling places. However, would they stay in the area and be counted in the census? The rents paid by those living along First Avenue have dropped relatively from their 1950 level and are slightly lower than rents in Belltown and higher than rents in the Pioneer Square census tract and International District. The percentage of men aged 14 or over and not in the labor force was highest of anywhere in Seattle in 1970 in the census tract that included First Avenue downtown. First Avenue is the area with the densest concentration of pawn shops, adult bookstores, penny arcades, and military-surplus stores in Seattle, and as such it attracts mostly male clientele and residents. While different from Skid Row, First Avenue clearly has provided and continues to provide facilities and services that Skid Row has traditionally required, which makes it part of Skid Row.

The CBD of Seattle does not contain a great deal of upper-class housing. The housing and labor-force characteristics therein come mainly from the zone just outside the CBD. This area includes the entertainment strip on Pike Street. Many commercial enterprises bordering Pike Street are but one class up from, and of the same genre as, those along First Avenue. Consistently having a high proportion of renters over the last few decades, the CBD has shifted from an above-median-rent area to a below-median-rent area. However, since 1960 the sex ratio has decreased. The percentage of men not in the labor force has increased only slightly more than that for the city as a whole. With the median number per household barely above the level for Skid Row census tracts, the minimum possible median, the CBD is in large part an area of single people. However, even with a relatively declining rent rate, the low sex ratio and the relatively low percentage of men not in the labor force indicate that the census tract including Pike Street from Fifth Street to Ninth Street is apparently not becoming a Skid Row–like area.

The Upper Pike area, northeast of the CBD, is similar in characteristics to the CBD in that it has been primarily a rental district, though ownership is increasing. The area has had and maintains a very low sex ratio. Its rents have been relatively declining, though only in 1970 did they become less than the median rent in Seattle. The median number per household is low, and in 1970 the percentage of men not in the labor force was somewhat higher than in earlier decades. Overall, given this evidence, the area around Pike Street just east of Interstate 5 is not Skid Row–like and shows few signs of becoming so.

International District, with its Oriental restaurants and food stores, its pagoda-shaped park shelters and Oriental businesses, has the lowest median rent in the city of Seattle and the highest percentage of renter-occupied housing units. International District is second only to the First Avenue area in percentage of men over age 14 not in the labor force. It also has a high sex ratio, though decreasing, and a very low median number of persons per households. International District has demographic characteristics similar to Skid Row, and indeed it has served and still serves a population of Skid Row men in addition to the Chinese, Japanese, Philippine, and other people who may be seen on its busy streets.

The Pioneer Square area in 1970 was still a bastion of Skid Row characteristics. The area is at the southern end of the CBD between the First Avenue area on the northwest and International District on the east. It is the historical Skid Road with all the traditions and color thereof. The area has been consistently at or near the extreme in almost every census indicator of Skid Row-ness. The one exception is in percentage of men over age 14 and not in the labor force, in which category, although high, Pioneer Square has a lower percentage than other census tracts having a high count of Skid Row indicators. Because of the loss of buildings between 1950 and 1970 and their replacement with nonresidential buildings, and because of the continuation of this trend in the 1970s, the quantity of Skid Row-ness the Pioneer Square area once knew is highly unlikely to return. However, the composition of the remaining population is not changing much. Inexplicably, as it was for the First Avenue census tract, the Pioneer Square area had a very small number of housing units reported occupied in 1950. The population and median number per household that year make it likely that either an error exists in the reporting or a drastic unreported change in census-taking procedures has occurred.

South of Pioneer Square is a geographically quite large census tract that includes freight yards, warehouses, some businesses, and residential areas. This area and an adjacent census tract, which includes the area known as Georgetown, three-and-one-half miles south of the CDB, are not becoming more Skid Row-like.

Because the boundary shifted between the Georgetown census tract and the tract south of Pioneer Square, it is impossible to tell precisely what has happened. The Georgetown tract lost a parcel of land in 1970 that may have in part caused its Skid Row-ness to increase slightly. Georgetown decreased in Skid Row-like characteristics between 1950 and 1960 and then increased somewhat between 1960 and 1970. The tract south of the Pioneer Square-area census tract, while gaining territory from Georgetown, increased in Skid Row-ness on one variable, decreased on two, and held steady on two.

Striking changes for Georgetown are the large drop in sex ratio (from 194 to 95), the drop in population, and the large drop in median number of people per household, all occurring between 1950 and 1960. No other census tract discussed here saw such great changes in a decade during the period this study covers. Most striking for the tract south of Pioneer Square was the huge jump in percentage of Seattle median rent between 1960 and 1970, going from 64 percent to 114 percent. The census-tract-boundary shift and the moderate decrease in percentage of Seattle median rent in Georgetown do not account for the rent jump in the tract south of Pioneer Square. Considerable upgrading in the area is most likely the reason for the jump.

To summarize the Seattle census-tract data for the years 1950, 1960, and 1970, Belltown appears to be the area in Seattle most showing distinct changes toward Skid Row-like characteristics, but Belltown does not match the concentration of characteristics long seen in areas more known for their Skid Row population—for example, the Pioneer Square area, the First Avenue area, and to some extent International District. Though these areas have undergone drastic population decreases and decreases in number of housing units, their demographic characteristics indicative of a Skid Row life-style have not changed. Both the CBD and the area to the northeast, the upper Pike area, have a high proportion of rental housing, but they provide homes for more women than men. The CBD showed a drop in rent relative to other rents in Seattle, and the upper Pike area in 1970 recorded a sharp rise in number of men not in the labor force, but otherwise neither area indicates a change toward Skid Row-ness. Similarly, Ballard and Fremont show few signs of becoming more Skid Row-like. Georgetown increased in Skid Row characteristics somewhat, but this may have been in part because of a boundary rearrangement with the census tract south of Pioneer Square. The tract south of Pioneer Square showed clear movement on two variables away from Skid Row-ness.

Overall, a good sampling of areas around the CBD in Seattle has shown that over three census periods, one of these areas, Belltown, is clearly acquiring demographic characteristics approaching those of areas long considered to be Skid Row-like. Three longstanding Skid Row strongholds retain their characteristics, though with much reduced population. Six other areas, in varying degrees, are holding their own, but five of these six areas are showing some slippage in relative status.

Detox

The King County Alcoholic Treatment Facility—or, as it is commonly known, Detox—operates with the philosophy that the care the facility provides is based upon respect for the dignity and worth of the individual. The goals of the staff include providing patients with factual knowledge about the disease of alcoholism and creating and fostering an environment that is supportive and protective of the inebriated or alcoholic patient (Alcoholic

Treatment Facility Staff 1974). The treatment given at Detox includes medication to alleviate symptoms of withdrawal from alcohol and/or other drugs, treatment for other medical emergencies, and inspection for communicable diseases. The average length of stay during the first two years of the operation of Detox was 55 hours. The Detox program began on a pilot basis in 1974 and began operating 1 January 1975 with a capacity for treating several hundred patients per month. In keeping with the recommendation in the Uniform Act, a continuum of care is made available to each Detox client in the form of a referral to one of over twenty treatment facilities that have programs lasting from twenty-one to ninety days.

Treatment at Detox begins with referral to a hospital-screening procedure. In 1975 when the program began, sources of referral to this screening were self-referral, 39 percent; police, 21 percent; ambulance, 13 percent; friends, 7 percent; family, 4 percent; and other, 15 percent. In 1976, an emergency patrol was created. The patrol picks up the acutely intoxicated in public places, with their consent, and is now the major source of referral to hospital screening. Around 80 percent of those screened in the first two years of Detox's operation were admitted.

The Detox service is not aimed exclusively at the Skid Row drunk, but the clientele utilizing the service are largely similar in characteristics to that of Skid Row missions (Fagan and Mauss 1978). In the first two years of Detox's operation, about 12 percent of the clientele paid the approximately $40-per-day cost of the services they received. Fagan and Mauss (1978) discovered that the number of admissions to Detox per year approximately equaled the number of police pickups for public drunkenness prior to the creation of Detox. The number of public drunks and the official management they require did not change markedly because of the creation of Detox. At least this was the case through the second year of Detox. In its first two years of operation, Detox admitted 6,792 clients a total of 21,718 times, an average of 3.2 admissions per client. Most clients, 63.7 percent, were admitted only once, and 22.2 percent were admitted from two to four times. Another 14.1 percent were admitted five or more times. Using this last category to define recidivism, Fagan and Mauss (1978) found four times as many recidivists under the Detox program as under the police handling of drunkenness. Additionally, 38 people were admitted to Detox over fifty times in the first two years of its operation.

Fagan and Mauss's (1978) assessment of the program is succinctly contained in the title of their article, "Padding the Revolving Door." The expectation of the Uniform Act, a decline in the classical revolving-door pattern—that is, the repeated processing of certain people for drunkenness—has not been realized. Since Detox is apparently not significantly affecting the level of Skid Row-ness by successfully referring Skid Row alcohol consumers to long-term treatment facilities—very few accept referral to any of the more than twenty facilities—and since the average stay in Detox is so short, the program cannot be said to be reducing Skid Row-ness.

For purposes of assessing the shifting location of Skid Row. the Detox records of the locations of pickups would not cover a sufficiently long period of time to permit longitudinal comparison, and the records, the author was told, were not readily available. However, an interview with the driver of the Detox Emergency Patrol van in August 1978 revealed that the most frequent location of pickups was the vicinity of the Pike Street Public Market, near the border between the First Avenue area and Belltown. A second location of frequent pickups identified by the driver was Occidental Square, which is in the Pioneer Square area. The driver also reported that since 1975 there had been a notable increase in the number of young people he picked up, including a growing proportion of women.

Street Questionnaire

The questioning of 127 men in the Skid Row areas of Seattle in 1972 and 1973 included a question about where they thought most of the men living in the area would go if the older hotels (for example, the Puget Sound Hotel) kept getting closed up. The interviewer was instructed to probe for at least one specific place. "I don't know," or something equivalent, was the most frequent response, 55.2 percent. Belltown was the response of 19 percent. Other Northwest cities were the choice of 12.6 percent, and International District , Ballard, the missions, and U.S. cities other than those in the Northwest were each mentioned by one or two respondents. Of the areas of interest in this study, only Belltown, International District, and Ballard are mentioned, and only Belltown received any substantial proportion of the votes of the Skid Row-area men as the likely spot for "most guys living around here" to go. The perception of the man on the street is consistent with other data we have seen.

Conclusion

As a summary of all of the data, we can say that the decline of Skid Row characteristics in Seattle in the 1970s has continued in the pattern of the 1950s and 1960s. The population and the buildings in the Skid Row areas are still being replaced by higher-class commercial enterprises. Belltown, at the northwest end of the CBD, appears to hae been the only area that has acquired characteristics of Skid Row since the 1950 census. Belltown has shown the greatest increase in the number and proportion of men disaffiliated from their families. It is also the most frequent response of Skid Row-area interviewees asked where displaced Skid Row men might go.

Public drinking may be increasing in Belltown, but the obvious derelicts largely remain in the Pioneer Square area. The institutions serving Skid Row men are disappearing from Belltown as fast as they are disappearing from all of the areas under study. The Pioneer Square area, the traditional Skid Road, still has most of the missions, and while decreasing drastically in resident population, it remains the hard-core Skid Row of Seattle. However, the Pioneer Square area is by no means visually dominated by Skid Row as it was twenty-five years ago and earlier. International District and the First Avenue area both contain institutions necessary to Skid Row—cheap housing, taverns, and retail and entertainment establishments catering to the working class—and generate a substantial portion of all measurements of Skid Row-ness. Both show declines in Skid Row-ness comparable to the overall Seattle decline, though International District shows some increase after 1975 in frequency of observations of Skid Row indicators. Tacoma's Skid Row area, generalizing only from the street data, shows a decline between 1972 and 1978 virtually identical to the composite decline observed in areas under study in Seattle. The small outlying Seattle areas covered in the street observations and census figures, and the CBD and the other areas around the CBD for which census data were presented, show no increase in Skid Row-ness. Pike Street and Ballard even show clear declines. The small cities on the Washington coast that theoretically might have absorbed the decline in Seattle and Tacoma had a few Skid Row institutions and in each a few Skid Row transitory variables were observed, but none of these small cities showed any possibility of developing a Skid Row area as such.

So what happens when the Skid Row has been knocked down and hauled away? The die-hards still hang around. The new recruits fit in somewhere—some settle in traditional areas and others disperse elsewhere. Detox makes life easier. In the war between the rich and the poor, the battle of Skid Row has been won by the rich. The undisputed turf of the Skid Row poor in Seattle is down to a very few spots, and then only at certain times.

5

Convincing Citizens, Politicians, and Other Scientists

Scientific interests, in the purest sense, are simply aimed at convincing citizens, politicians, and other scientists that certain theories or discoveries are true and should be accepted as such. . . . It is also important to keep in mind that scientists do not always speak (or write) from the point of view of their scientific interests alone. Scientists, like other citizens, may promote economic, political, moral, or other interests, and when they do so they are not entitled to any special credibility just because they happen to be scientists.
—Mauss and Wolfe (1977, p. 13)

Thus far, we have examined Skid Row as an urban neighborhood and as a way of life. We have seen that a number of interests have historically been pitted against the very existence of Skid Row, most often without notable success. For social and economic reasons, Skid Row has declined in prominence both as a way of life and as an urban neighborhood. However, the precipitous decline of the physical plant of Skid Row neighborhoods in recent decades has probably outstripped the natural decline in population. This is true in part because of continuing recruitment to the Skid Row lifestyle. To some decree the Skid Row population has been displaced, and this displacement raised the question of the present and future location of Skid Row. We have sought the answer in a variety of theories of urban development and process. To empirically resolve the question, using Seattle, Washington, as a case study, we developed a multifarious measurement scheme utilizing a unique Skid Row–ness scale, Seattle Police Department data, King County Medical Examiner data, census data, information from the Seattle Alcohol Treatment Facility (Detox), and interviews with 127 Skid Row men. We have yet to assess the theories, examine policy implications, or objectively examine the place of this work in the context of the literature on Skid Row.

Data Review

A brief review of the yields from the various data sources may aid in assessing the theories. The street data showed a decline of Skid Row characteristics between 1972 and 1978. Notable was the continuing presence of transitory items in the Pioneer Square area even with a decrease in Skid Row institutions comparable to the overall decline in such institutions. Some increase in transitory-item observations was recorded for Belltown. The periphery blocks of the areas covered by the street data showed less decline than did the more-central blocks. Police data were used in two forms—aggregate statistics and individuals' records. The aggregate arrest statistics show a sharp decrease in number of arrests for charges typical of Skid Row corresponding to the phasing in of Detox. An increasing percentage of arrests for Skid Row–type offenses was observed in the Pioneer Square area. The highest percentage of such arrests consistently was registered in the commercial First Avenue area. Individual arrest records show that most people who are arrested there do not live in the Skid Row area. These "rap sheets" also pinpoint areas in the city away from Skid Row that are apparently frequented by Skid Row men. These records do not show any change in downtown-area arrest locations. The medical examiner's records of unclaimed bodies show that Belltown registered the only substantial increase of any Skid Row area. The only other area with a noteworthy rise was the area from one to two miles from the CBD. The totals in the two comparison years, 98 and 79 respectively for 1971–1972 and 1977–1978, are too small to be strong evidence, but Skid Row growth in Belltown and general dispersion are the implications. The census data from 1950 to 1970 show long-term growth in Skid Row characteristics only in Belltown. The other Skid Row areas, while losing their population, had not, as of 1970, been residentially populated by any class different from Skid Row people. They retain their Skid Row demographic characteristics. The Detox data show that the program has not reduced Skid Row–ness. Rather, it has made the treatment of public inebriates more humane. The Skid Row questionnaire shows that Belltown is the only area Skid Row men see as the likely roost for those displaced from closing hotels. In summary, Belltown is the only area increasing in Skid Row characteristics, but evidence of Belltown's increase is not dramatic and does not include increases in all indicators of Skid Row–ness. The Pioneer Square area retains the greatest proportion of Skid Row behavior. Skid Row thus continues to decline as an urban neighborhood in Seattle.

The Hypotheses

Given this data summary, if the reader refers to table 2-2 first then table 2-1, we can examine the hypotheses and then each of the theories. The hypothesis shown in table 2-2 as the strongest—gradual dispersal—is in large part borne out in reality. If recruitment to Skid Row continues, and if demolition and renovation have occurred at a faster pace than the pace of natural decline in the existing Skid Row population, then the decreases we have recorded mean that Skid Row has largely been dispersed.

The second strongest hypothesis, according to the theories reviewed, is the prediction of a relatively intact shift to a single similar distinct area. This has not happened though this hypothesis is far more supported than the hypotheses predicting other shifts. Virtually no shift has occurred to satellite skid rows or to hinterland skid rows; at least observations made in the course of this study located none. Belltown is the area receiving any noteworthy shift in location of Skid Row-ness, but it is also declining in Skid Row-ness as registered on some indicators.

The third strongest hypothesis—disappearance of Skid Row altogether as a distinct area—is somewhat difficult to assess. The direction is toward disappearance, but surges in street-data totals indicate possibilities for revival. Casual observation comparing 1950 with 1980 might lead one to believe that disappearance was imminent, but the United States has experienced thirty increasingly prosperous years, with only minor fluctuations. Even today, congregate Skid Row behavior is easily observable. The staying power of Skid Row over the decades further encourages caution in taking for granted the disappearance of Skid Row as a distinct area.

The Theories

Let us look then at the theories individually and see which best describes reality as we have found it. The reader may refer to table 2-1 for a summary of each of the following theorists or theories. Beginning at the top, Quinn appears to be partially correct in predicting dispersal and quite correct in predicting the clustering of Skid Row around services, but he is incorrect in predicting disappearance. The continued centering of Skid Row in the Pioneer Square area, clustering around the missions, is the reason Quinn's second prediction is right. The disappearance prediction assumes a continuing decrease in functional importance. Given the nature of Skid Row as reviewed in chapter 1, we can only guess, with the projected inflation and decreasing availability of petroleum, whether casual labor will experience a resurgence of demand.

Hawley is partially wrong on one count and clearly right on another. First, arguing that the physical plant of Skid Row—the natural area—is necessary for the behavioral aspects of Skid Row is at least partially in error as shown in the Pioneer Square-area findings. The institutions, other than the missions, have disappeared faster than the transistory items. Elsewhere, Hawley may be right, as increases and decreases in transitory scores tended to follow similar changes in institutional scores rather than vice versa. On the second count—identifying the stability of a symbiotic relationship—

Hawley is right. The men and the missions remain in the Pioneer Square area.

Burgess predicts that Skid Row will remain in the zone immediately adjacent to the CBD, shifting if dispersed to another area in this zone. He is essentially correct. Skid Row remains largely in the Pioneer Square area, and what shift is recorded is to Belltown, also in this area.

Hoyt's sector theory would have a dispersed Skid Row move outward in the same quadrant. This would have shifted the Pioneer Square–area concentration into International District or into the area south of Pioneer Square, but neither has happened. Furthermore, contrary to Hoyt's prediction, Belltown, where some of the shifting Skid Row–ness landed, is moderately uphill from Pioneer Square.

Harris and Ullman's satellite Skid Row prediction did not materialize. While there are satellite attraction points, the range of opportunities for Skid Row men is not, or has not been, sufficient to promote migration on a noticeable scale. This is true at least in the two locations that knowledgeable observers named as possible satellite Skid Rows, Fremont and Ballard.

Stouffer predicts dispersal as opportunities dwindle, and this, in fact, has happened. Transitory-item changes in an area tend to follow institutional-item changes rather than vice versa. This is not entirely so in the Pioneer Square area, where Skid Row behavior increases while institutional opportunities decline. However, important opportunities, the missions, remain in the Pioneer Square area, as does much of the Skid Row population. Stouffer, if highly general, is mostly right.

Brown and Moore tie Skid Row location to housing and predict dispersal with a decrease in housing supply. This has happened. Skid Row housing is much diminished. However, housing is to a degree dissociated from Skid Row as is evidenced in "rap-sheet" data. People who frequent Skid Row are largely people who do not live in the immediate area.

Hawley's views on advanced communication, combined with Schmid's identification of Ballard and Fremont and other sources who named the same places as areas where Skid Row men went prior to 1972, do not accurately predict the emergence of satellite Skid Rows. Either more than communication is necessary or perhaps the pioneers who happened upon these areas did not discover sufficient merit to communicate to other prospective migrants. Lack of any communication at all is unlikely given the proportion of the typical Skid Row man's day that is spent in casual conversation.

Rose's low-status-invader theory has not worked yet, but it could in Belltown. The long-term changes there, as identified in census data, could continue to attract Skid Row men. Properties in Belltown could be allowed to become run down. Businesses could start vacating premises, and a dramatic change could occur. Whether Skid Row in Seattle has sufficient stigma attached to it and whether the numbers of Skid Row people are sufficient to induce the panic-driven vacating behavior for a succession of the population to occur is questionable.

Roebuck, in predicting the least expensive area as the likely spot for displaced poor, does not take into consideration other needs and preferences of the poor. International District is the least expensive area in which to live, yet no great Skid Row influx has occurred there. Probably some of the very least expensive habitats are not even in the city, yet Skid Row has always been and probably will continue to be an urban phenomenon. It is likely, however, that the poor, including the Skid Row poor, will continue to live in inexpensive housing. Most of the housing around the CBD is the lowest cost housing in the city, except for low-income housing projects. This is an area not included in this study. As this author understands from casual reading, housing projects mainly house blacks and families. Displaced Skid Row people may be simply paying more for housing than they did when more housing was available near the CBD.

Cooley links rents to transportation costs, and transportation costs are rising. Rents should rise, and this will drive out marginal businesses. Skid Row contains many marginal businesses, and these are likely to fold, according to Cooley, unless some technological or organizational breakthrough causes transporation costs to go down. Transporation costs have been rising dramatically in the 1970s, rents have been going up, and marginal Skid Row enterprises have been going out of business. Skid Row, however, was being dispersed some years before gasoline began its precipitous tripling in price between 1972 and 1980. Skid Row was declining in the 1960s when the suburbanization of the country was in full swing and incredibly cheap transportation was available. It seems that variables other than transportation are more effective in precipitating the decline of Skid Row.

Guttenberg offers a unique prediction based on the mode of transportation utilized by Skid Row men. Because Skid Row men walk most places, Skid Row will not expand. In this he is correct, as the data show. Skid Row has remained fairly compact. This undoubtedly helps explain why the missions have remained clustered in the Pioneer Square area. To relocate might put them outside the convenient transportation range of many walkers. Guttenberg's theory would also predict that if Skid Row were displaced, it would shift intact.

Firey's cultural-ecology theory is right in identifying cultural factors as casual. They way in which cultural values are manifest is not, however, as inferred in table 2–1—that is, the negative cultural values associated with Skid Row have not yet helped Skid Row to successfully invade another area. Instead, apparently, cultural values have kept Skid Row in its traditional spot. Institutional support, other than by the missions, for skid row men, has declined considerably in the Pioneer Square area. Why the missions have stayed, and why Skid Row men, not all of whom utilize the missions, have stayed seems best explained in terms of cultural values. Skid Row, or Skid Road, is where persons who are more or less permanently loitering feel quite in place. Cultural values are not alone, however, in keeping Skid Road put. With the missions, material considerations may well have much influence on their collective decision to remain in the Pioneer Square area. Even those that are strictly charitable and that do not take in money must show some supporting organization that they are fulfilling their purpose of serving the downtrodden. Many men undoubtedly frequent the Pioneer Square area because of the services the missions provide. Underlying this symbiotic, circular-support arrangement, one may still infer a sense that ideals rather than material considerations predominate in the collective choice to keep Skid Road as Skid Row.

Social engineering, in this case the concerted effort to eliminate Skid Row by removing or upgrading Skid Row buildings and flooding residents with services designed to remove them from the category of Skid Row man, has been successful only in the first goal of eliminating Skid Row buildings. Financial support for the second goal was not forthcoming, whether or not it could possibly have been reached. Millions, perhaps billions, of dollars were spent on the demolition and renovation of Skid Row buildings in the United States, much as social engineers who agreed upon the nature of urban renewal had planned. Social-service hopes and plans materialized in the war on poverty, but most of the benefits to the poor could not be utilized by the typical Skid Row man. Rehabilitation from alcoholism was his benefit. That benefit became manifest in Seattle with the creation of Detox and the longer-term programs to which the Skid Row drunk is referred but to which he seldom goes. Social engineering, as it specifically related to Skid Row, essentially amounted to destroying the residential nature of the area and providing a softer place to land following a drunken spree.

The best prediction that can be gleaned from the theories as a whole and from their correspondence, or lack of it, to reality is that Belltown is likely to continue to grow as a Skid Row area. If the transition of Belltown were to accelerate, it could lead to an exodus of the missions and other Skid Row–support facilities from the Pioneer Square area. However, the history of Skid Road may figure prominently in keeping Skid Row in the Pioneer Square area, as may facilities far more permanent than the organizations serving Skid Row—namely, the public squares and parks in the Pioneer Square area, which are very casual, comfortable places for Skid Row men.

Policy Implications

The policy choices for the city of Seattle are clear. First, Skid Row can be allowed to remain in the Pioneer Square area through tolerance of the missions, other organizations, and the men. Second, the missions can be invited in various positive ways to move to Belltown, after which Skid Row behaviors would surely follow. Third, continued pressure through code enforcement can continue to carry out the plan of Skid Row eradication. Whether there is a lower limit beyond which the characteristics of Skid Row cannot be driven is a question that has not yet been tested. There may be. This third alternative has been pursued, not directly by the city of Seattle, but through the Washington State Department of Social and Health Services. Suit was brought against the Union Gospel Mission to make it conform to state hotel regulations. The mission contended it was not a hotel but a charitable shelter for the poor and alcoholic. Had the Department of Social and Health Services won the case, the Union Gospel Mission, the largest in the state, and all other missions would probably have been forced to incur considerable additional expenses (Ruppert 1979, p. C16). The mission won the case, however. Not only do the agents of the government affect the future of Skid Row but also the mission personnel, businessmen (bar and store owners), and police officers, acting as individual persons, all have some influence. Real estate interests are certainly not powerless in the matter. However, the official position of government at various levels wields the shaping mallet.

Broader policy implications relate to the nature of Skid Row itself. A society must manage its vagrants and derelicts in one way or another. The geographic area known as Skid Row was one such management arrangement, although perhaps natural rather than arranged, as the term *management* might imply. What does the dispersal of Skid Row mean? What conditions exist for vagrants and derelicts now that the geographic area of Skid Row no longer contains them?

The answer has been put forth in what Bahr (1978, p. xi) calls "a significant conceptual change in the definition of Skid Row." The reconceptualization is that of Blumberg, Shipley, and Barsky (1978), whose book, *Liquor and Poverty: Skid Row as a Human Condition,* Bahr introduces. After an unsuccessful search for locations to which the Philadelphia Skid Row might be shifting, using a few indicators identical to those on the Skid Row-ness scale developed in this study (their efforts were briefly discussed in chapter 4), Blumberg's group propose to treat Skid Row-ness (their term) as a human condition, a continuum on which we all fall somewhere, rather than as it has been treated historically, as a geographical area:

[T]o limit research and ameliorative efforts to only the residential Skid Rows is to be shortsighted and to miss the point which has become so evident—that Skid Row is not just a residential area with a characteristic collection of agencies within and surrounding it. Skid Row is a characteristic of people within our society. It is a complex of poverty, powerlessness, alienation, homelessness, and perhaps, alcohol or drug addiction, for which we are all eligible to a greater or lesser degree. [Blumberg, Shipley, and Barsky 1978, pp. 121–122]

These investigators explicitly offer justification for their reconceptualization of Skid Row as people (with liquor and poverty) rather than as an area by examining populations that include people with Skid Row–like characteristics but who are not, at present at least, occupying an area commonly known as Skid Row. These populations are blacks, women, the urban poor, and wanderers. Blacks with Skid Row–like characteristics live in small sections of black neighborhoods. Women with such characteristics live in rooming houses in low-income sections of the city. The urban poor, who live in many areas, everywhere includes a proportion of persons who live in a Skid Row life-style.

Wanderers appear to be largely a new breed on the U.S. scene. In looking at various types of wanderers, Blumberg and his co-workers discuss the history of the Haight Ashbury area in San Francisco that lead to the area's occupation by the so-called hippies in the 1960s. Following the hippies came the so-called street people, a category that usually refers to young people who are mostly of working-class origin and who are dropouts from stable, productive, community-bound circumstances. Their characteristics, except for youth and sex ratio (about 20 percent female), are much like the traditional Skid Row population. From a knowledgeable San Francisco source, an author of two publications on street people (Baumahl 1973; Baumahl and Miller 1974), the Blumberg group obtained the estimates that about 5,000 street people pass through the San Francisco Bay area in a year and that as many as a million of them may be in the United States. The street people congregate in university areas and interact with the same institutions as university-related residents of the youth ghetto. However, they are not friendly with the university descendants of the "flower children," and the students, in fact, seem to be afraid of the street population. A second category of wanderers that Blumberg, Shipley, and Barsky discuss is people in flight. These people are usually older than the street people and are fleeing from situations they consider intolerable. They are usually caught in a web of problems. They set off with no plans of support and seek aid at points of crisis. Their flights tend to occur repeatedly, and economic hard times increase the number of such people in flight.

Blumberg and his associates recognize that in classic terminology the people they term *street people* and *people in flight* have been called *vagrants*. They conclude

It seems likely that out of the most "flighty" will come persons who ultimately "perch" more or less permanently in Skid Row areas or who will be found among the Skid Row–like residents of the poor sections of the big cities when, and if, Skid Row areas themselves disappear. [Blumberg, Shipley, and Barsky et al., 1978, p. 174]

While the Blumberg group would change the conceptualization of Skid Row from primarily an area to primarily a human condition, they still refer, as in the preceding quotation and elsewhere, to a congregation of people, activities, and institutions in a central area known as Skid Row.

The point made by these researchers is well taken. However, Skid Row *is* a geographical collection of a type of people, activities, and organizations and has been for over a century in this country. Its location is problematic in affairs of urban governments and businesses, not to mention people offended by the squalor and degradation that Skid Row displays. Skid Row is an entity that occupies urban territory, and it is not the invisible poor that Harrington (1963) described. It is quite visible, though declining in prominence. While we are grateful to Blumberg, Shipley, and Barsky for expanding the meaning of Skid Row, we must continue to consider Skid Row in the traditional sense as well because it is in part the concentration of Skid Row people that makes them of concern to policymakers.

Solutions

There is no doubt that we are far from the solution to the problem of Skid Row. Still, a brief parting shot is perhaps in order. Blumberg, Shipley, and Barsky (1978) suggest that the solution is for society to simply put up with people who cannot or will not work regularly. They suggest a multistory village complete with liquor store, in which Skid Row–like persons could live and where all services would be available. The diametrically opposite solution is to provide no publicly supported facilities for vagrants, derelicts, or other able-bodied people. In a belt-tightening society, as we apparently are, the first alternative is unlikely on a mass scale. The second alternative would at times be a severe hardship for large numbers of people, especially Skid Row people. Such cutbacks would be likely to cause civil unrest, a rash of crime, or both if some alternative way to get sustenance were not immediately available. A third alternative, the most likely one, is continuing as we are with the missions, the service centers, drop-in centers, emergency shelters, and Detox. No clearly superior alternative for the present time appears to this writer.

Should conditions change and force large numbers into the ranks of the unemployed, then operations can be expanded, if necessary, to the scale of refugee camps. In this mechanized, freedom-loving land, it just would not do to propose productive, labor-intensive operations such as the rural communes of the People's Republic of China as a model for relieving U.S. urban areas of a nonproductive population. However, similar rural enterprises could be designed to productively accommodate varying numbers of people of varied levels of ability, free to come and go. With a status structure designed to promote effort and tenure, such largely independent associations could, after an initial bankrolling, become financially independent. The concept of a commune for transients might well appeal to the street people; to others, perhaps and perhaps not.

Critique

Perhaps the major scientific and social-policy contribution of this work lies in the development of the Skid Row–ness scale. It is unique as a method whereby immediate updating of indicators of a persistent urban phenomenon can be obtained at short and regular intervals, without having to wait for the publication of official records like the census and police data. Another contribution of the study is its testing of some implications of certain theories. Perhaps our results and further questions arising from this work will lead to a better understanding of urban processes. Furthermore, substantive knowledge about the nature and extent of Skid Row in Seattle has been produced through the application of several diverse data sources brought to bear on some questions. Has this work done any good otherwise?

Identifying people who sadly spend their days surreptitiously swigging wine, watching the traffic, and urinating in the alley as mere scores on a scale, as cases of a transitory variable, or as elements of Skid Row–ness is not very humanistic. Treating the death of a person who was alone and without family as just another pin on a map pushes into the background the sadness and pity such circumstances naturally evoke. Deep philosophical insight into the human condition does not seem to be part of such quantitative callousness. Neither empathy nor sympathy has played much of a part in this study. The fact that people live alone under debasing circumstances and that some of them destroy their capacities in an alcoholic haze, debilitating their bodies and poisoning their minds, is only remotely related to the statement, "Skid Row–ness is up slightly in 1978." How can counting and mapping help the poor victim of the Skid Row life? How can it promote what is good and just? What values justify the time and effort expended in this numerary exercise?

This problem is stated in a critical tone, but it need not be. The philosophical arena within which this study is located is not axiology or metaphysics, but epistemology. A sufficient justification of this study lies in a belief in science as the way to truth. This study follows the scientific pattern of wonder → theory → hypothesis → data gathering → analysis → conclusion. Scientifically, the methods are explicit, and one hopes they are clear. This may all add up to value-free science, but the question remains why?

To some extent, we have addressed why and related issues elsewhere (Montague and Miller 1974). Here we might say simply that we advocate not only a love of learning but also a love of the practical products of learning. Knowledge is power. William Harvey discovered the circulation of blood. Louis Pasteur discovered the role of the microorganism in disease. Albert Einstein discovered the nature of the atom. The truth in these matters had certain consequences for the conduct of human affairs. Can we be so ambitious with social knowledge? We can treat and tamper with a human body medically. We can manipulate the atom with seeming impunity. Can we manipulate society? We do. Studies of educational achievement led rather directly to enforced busing of students to achieve racial balance in schools. The labeling theory of deviant behavior led rather directly to processing delinquent youths in so-called diversion programs to avoid the stigma of contact with the police. However, the manipulation of people by people goes on with or without sociology. Sociology and the scientific knowledge it generates about social conditions and variables, we hope, make more sensitive and intelligent the manipulation that occurs.

Ultimately, the justification of scientific sociology, even if apparently nonhumanistic, lies in its functional role in the establishment and preservation of society as a tolerable and rewarding condition of life. Otherwise, sociology is a hollow science for science's sake or perhaps even a chic art for art's sake. To that functional end is made the offering of knowledge this effort generates.

The aspiration to high-level functional purposes aside, sociology is also a sensitizing discipline, bringing to consumers new concepts and awareness of social systems beyond their own. In this role, sociology is somewhat akin to journalism. Journalists are perhaps less concerned with the mundane aspects of social life. Just how a social system is maintained on a day-to-day basis is of central interest to ethnographic sociologists as well as cultural anthropologists. In chapter 6, I attempt to convey a sense of the day-to-day life of some of the people I met during the course of this study.

6 One of the Paths

Complementary to the study in composite facts and abstract figures, a straightforward telling of what I experienced will expose the reader to the raw data of Skid Row. In this chapter I share with you the most ethnographically valid experience of those I can recall, where I best came to know the meaning of the disaffiliated life.

While it would be possible for me to describe nights shared with wheezing bunkmates in Seattle missions, various characters I have met, or bottle-gang experiences, I could only do so in a limited, distant way. My participation in the life of Skid Row was limited. Except for two occasions, I avoided bottle gangs as an unhealthy sharing of microorganisms. I never begged. I ate in missions after services several times, but only on two occasions did I spend a night in a mission. My usual view of Skid Row—for example, nosing into doorways after discarded bottles or watching three fellows to see if they would pass a bottle so I could count them as a bottle gang—did not lend itself to developing personal ties with Skid Row people. I certainly saw great numbers of people that looked like they might be interesting to get to know, but except for the first year I was always on a schedule and in a hurry.

While Skid Row did not absorb me, one of the traditional paths to Skid Row did—tramping. The occupation of the tramp involves working temporary, usually not high-skill jobs in different places in the country at different times of the year. It involves a lot of traveling. Migrant families usually drive automobiles. Tramps sometimes do, but most low-paid tramps do not, preferring freights and other public transportation.

The days of railroad building were the heyday of the tramp. Decades since have seen decline, and the most precipitous tapering of the tramp traffic occurred in the early 1960s, concurrent with the rapid decline of Skid Row. The sector of the job market that tramps fill has diminished but still exists, and so does a tramp subculture.

The study of Skid Row in Seattle brought me into casual contact with men who spoke about riding freight trains. Such information seemed to have little to do with my study, except to suggest that emergent Skid Row areas would probably locate near railroad tracks. I had not seriously considered riding a freight myself until I moved from Washington State to Grand

Forks, North Dakota. The University of North Dakota, in Grand Forks, is adjacent to the Burlington Northern Railroad switchyard. During a break from desk work, I was walking near the English Coulee (River) where it flows under the tracks when a switch engine stopped about 50 yards away. The engineer in shirt-sleeves had waved as he went by. I thought about getting to Seattle and walked down the track to the engine. I asked the engineer how difficult it would be to ride a freight to Seattle. The answer came in terms of the numbers of the trains leaving Grand Forks and concluded with the advice to ask at the yard office. The engineer was not discouraging, but the definite feasibility of the trip was not obvious either. I had in mind that railroad people at least frowned on free riders.

Following up two days later, I asked a man near the roundhouse, presumably a railroad employee, where I could find out when trains left. He directed me to the yardmaster's office. I walked there and asked the first person I saw, just inside the door, how a poor man could best get to Seattle. This man suggested going to Fargo and catching the Symbol (or Cymbal, I do not know which) that goes directly to Seattle with stops only to change crews. He also cautioned me to be sure to take water along, because it is a long haul and there will not be a chance to get any along the way. He said a train would leave for Fargo in the morning and that I should check with someone in the yard about departure time. The feasibility of such a trip was thus assured.

I had the flu the day I had planned to leave so I went back in the evening to enquire again and found that another train would leave the following morning. A man in the office asked if I were a student. I said I was, and he said to be careful.

The next morning, with backpack and two canteens, I again asked about the train to Fargo. The train was pointed out, and I was told it would leave within the hour. I walked across all the tracks to the other side of the yard and saw two men sitting there—tramps, those romanticized and maligned legendary fellows of the volumes of Skid Row literature I had read. I stopped to talk to them.

One was an American Indian about 40 years old, well dressed, healthy looking. The other was white, about 45, dressed in not-so-well-fitting clothes, and not particularly healthy looking. His face was red and he had wine sores on his forehead and lip (wine sores are cuts, abrasions, or lesions that do not heal normally, and they are attributed to heavy drinking over an extended period). They were both going east to Crookston. I said I was going to Fargo and told them which train was going there. No train to Crookston was due for a long time so they decided maybe they would go to Fargo. Then we talked some more. In a short time I was asked if this was the first time I had ridden the freights. The asker was fooled, he said, by my pack that was covered with a very old piece of canvas and tied in a strange

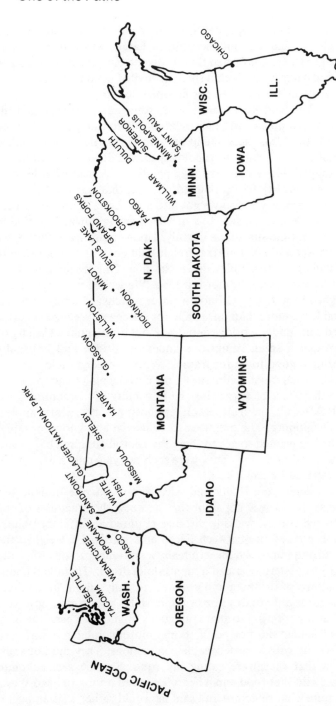

Figure 6–1. Northwest United States and Selected Railroad Towns

manner with very old cotton rope, definitely not a modern backpacker's rig. I asked a switchman again about the train to Fargo, which just had had more cars added to it. He confirmed that it was the one going to Fargo and that it would be leaving soon. With a smile he invited us to pick ourselves a coach. The three of us then looked for an open boxcar.

I was happy. The Skid Row literature has some nasty stories about the railroad "bulls" (yard police) and their relationship to tramps, but I found now that it is not so, at least here and at present. As the three of us walked alongside the train, an official grey car slowly moved down the road beside the tracks. It stopped, moved on, and then passed us. A man of at least 60 nodded and we waved. My friend pointed out that that was the "bull."

We found no open boxcars so we got into a gondola, an open steel car with four-foot-high walls, the side two of which swing down. The ride to Fargo was breezy, but the sun shone warmly. Upon enquiring in Fargo, we found that the westbound hotshot (fast freight) did not stop in Fargo but in Dilworth, a small town five miles down the line. Our discussion about whether or not to walk there did not last long. We waited until evening in Fargo and caught a local train to Minot, a major switchyard where hotshots are made up and leave more than once daily for the coast. We heated coffee water in charred cans under a bridge and drank out of the same. The city of Fargo had provided a small campstove under the bridge and is usually spoken of as being a good town for tramps. We ate some granola and raisins I had brought. In discussing itineraries, my definite plan to go to Seattle seemed to have the effect of suggesting the possibility of my companions' also going west. After all, the fruit season (apricots, peaches, pears, apples, and so on) was beginning. The pair seemed congenial and knowledgeable, and I offered, if they wanted to go, to share my bedroll (sleeping bag, blanket, and heavy canvas) and food. They were each carrying only a one-gallon plastic jug of water and a small sack.

My friends' names were Frank and Alec. Frank was the Indian, and from his conversation, it was apparent that he knew the schedules of the trains. He discussed routes, walking distance required at different points, and different job possibilities between Fargo and Seattle. He weighed the alternatives aloud and impressed me as a realistic, rational person. Alec, the white man, had just yesterday ended a month-long drunk. He talked about the stupidity and evil of drinking and groaned, literally, about how miserable he felt. His pains did not disguise or diminish his strong gait, however.

The idea that my offering to share my goods might have been the only reason I was befriended did not occur to me until much later. I was very happy to be traveling with knowledgeable companions. They did not seem to be concerned that they were eating my food. Sharing seemed quite natural. Alec had said that food and a bedroll were all it took to head West, but Frank was somewhat reluctant and said he would rather wait and get a bedroll. Alec clarified his commitment to travel with information about a warrant for his arrest in Fargo. He was supposed to have been a witness. He complained that it was not fair that he had already given a signed statement, so he should not have to appear. He would have appeared, he said, except he got drunk and slept through the trial. Mobile is the life of the tramp.

Frank suggested we go to a city facility that served a free evening meal. It was about three blocks from the tracks. Alec said he could not go there because he was barred three weeks ago for getting drunk and swearing at the man who runs the place. Frank and I walked there anyway, and I bought a fine, long-sleeved red-corduroy shirt for 25ᶜ in the secondhand-store part of the building. Outside, at the other end of the building near the entrance to the dining area, Frank met several men he knew, at least four or five out of the fifteen or so waiting there. These men were working at hoeing onions, and Frank decided to stay and do the same. One of the men expressed surprise that I was going to Seattle. He said there was nothing in Seattle, which meant no work.

The city facility was like a Salvation Army store and a Skid Row rescue mission combined, but without the chapel. There was a pool table, a TV room, magazines, sleeping area, kitchen, and serving area. The employees of the establishment ate in a partitioned-off area and had corn on the cob and other foods not served to the men I ate with. There were piles of day-old and older bakery goods and boxes of less than perfect produce, mainly fruit, in addition to the starchy but tasty broth, rolls, fruit, and peculiarly curdled milk served at the tables. I carried a shirtfull of food back to Alec. As I got ready to leave, Frank said to tell Alec that he would see him in Spokane in a week.

The train to Minot did not leave until around 10:00 P.M. Alec and I found a boxcar with one door open. We broke the seal on the other door with a rock and opened the door. Alec tossed in a fair-sized rock to scare away kids that sometimes pester tramps. Slight doubt and suspicion crossed my mind, but very slight. We also jammed a railroad spike into one door frame as assurance, in addition to the latch, that the door would not jam shut. Alec told of a time he had been drunk, sleeping in a car on a siding, when a jolt shut the door. Boxcars often are not opened for weeks and he had been pretty scared, but in the morning another tramp had opened the car. The fellow, who had been in the next car, had seen Alec get in the night before. This all sounded to me more like story than fact, but it certainly justified our cheap precaution. Alec also told of hearing of tramps' banging their heads on the end of boxcars following a quick stop, indicating that it was better to sleep sideways in the car. We slept right between the two open doors with the sleeping bag under, and the blanket and canvas over, us, a cool, jerky ride. I was not convinced that sleeping sideways is best. We were awakened at about 7:30 A.M. in Minot by a young fellow in a boxcar on the track next to the one on which our train stopped. He suggested we would appreciate being wakened, which we did. We enquired from a "brakey" (brakeman) about the hotshot going to Seattle. He told us which track it was making up on and that it would be leaving later in the morning. We moved to the side of the yard where several other tramps were, and we talked with them.

Conversation among tramps, like that at the Fargo soup kitchen, concerns jobs to be had in different parts of the country. Names of employers are traded along with stories of especially good deals. Information about places to get free meals, free clothes, free bedrolls, and money handouts is exchanged. Tips on railroad safety, stories about accidents, about crossing the Canadian border, news of the deaths of individuals, apparently other tramps, stories about fantastic occasions of earning or being given large amounts of money and spending it as fast or faster than it was earned, stories about tremendous drunken sprees—these all are told and probably retold elsewhere. Information about where the police are particularly down on tramps, where a young "bull" is tough on tramps in a particular yard, and about "slave camps" is offered and received attentively. A slave camp is a place where a farmer will come into town and advertise work at a certain rate than turns out to be misleading. For example, hoeing beans at $1.00 per row might sound reasonable, but the job could be 23 miles down a dirt road, and upon arriving, one might find that the rows are a half mile long. These farmers often have dogs to discourage workers from leaving. Workers also have to buy gloves and pay for food and lodging. If one does not drink wine, which can be purchased on credit, one can clear $2.00 to $4.00 per day (1975 dollars), a long day.

As the departure time of the big freight approached, more riders appeared. In all, in Minot, North Dakota, on Wednesday, 13 August 1975 at about 1:00 P.M., at least fifteen people other than railroad employees boarded the hotshot to Seattle. There were three women, each with a man. Their ages probably ranged from 20 to 30. The women were the object of some attention and surprise among the tramps I rode with. I inferred that women's riding was a recent if not also rare phenomenon. The men accompanying them had longish hair. Two men about 20 years old boarded a boxcar with ten-speed bicycles. We had seen them early in the morning in sleeping bags right under the three-story observation tower at the end of the switchyard. The rest of the passengers included a white-haired, crew-cut, pot-bellied, healthy-looking man of probably 55 (who I call Crew Cut); a 40-year-old man with a heavy New York accent and no teeth (called New Yorker); a 30–35-year-old thin black man with greying hair; the fellow who woke us, in his mid-twenties; and an abrasive 35-year-old man with yellow teeth. Alec offered the generalization that there were three sorts of people riding the freights—regular tramps, hippies, and Jesus people.

Alec and I had walked together and stood and sat together during the morning when we met most of the people on the train. We spent much of the morning in the company of Crew Cut and New Yorker, who had begun traveling together in Chicago. The four of us at one point smoothly but definitely ostracized the abrasive fellow because, as Alec remarked, "You never know what a guy like that will do."

There were several empty boxcars. Alec and I got one with a wood floor and both doors open. I new New Yorker and Crew Cut did not have food or a bedroll, just the ever-present gallon water jug and a small ($9'' \times 12'' \times 4''$) case. When we were looking over the cars, they were with Alec and me. I thought they were joining us (they had shared our food), but they took another, inferior car. I asked Alec if I should invite them to join us, and he said sure.

With probably ten heads bobbing in and out of doors (most of the empties were together), the hotshot to the coast clanked to the start of a day of scenic riding across the prairie. The two bicyclers got off first, in Montana. They had said they were cycling to the coast and had not wanted to pedal across the Dakotas (wind and no scenery). They had begun in Minneapolis, went to Willmar, Minnesota, to a major switchyard, and had ridden a freight from there to Minot the day before. Crew Cut got off in Harve, Montana, to work with a custom combine crew. While the brakemen inspected each set of wheels on the train, a process taking twenty-five minutes, Crew Cut had gone to a gas station and had heard that a combine crew had just come into town. Crew Cut tried to convince New Yorker that he should get off and work the wheat harvest, too, claiming one could make $40.00 per day. New Yorker refused, saying he knew nothing about farming and that he did not want to say he did and get fired the next day.

This incident of the parting of these two was not so simple. The train stopped in Havre, and most of the passengers got off and went to a water pipe near the center of the yard. I stayed in the car as did Crew Cut, but then he decided to go for cigarettes. Before leaving he told me that New Yorker had been wearing his clothes for over a week and smoking his cigarettes. He said he was going to put his clothes case by a nearby telephone pole in case he did not get back before the train pulled out. Soon New Yorker and Alec returned with water and noticed Crew Cut's absence. New Yorker badmouthed Crew Cut, claiming that the (terms deleted) scoundrel had run off with his clothes. I told him he just went for cigarettes and that he said he would be back, but New Yorker said that was ridiculous. Having traveled together as long as they had, he would have had no need to take the clothes case with him. It contained both their clothes. I then went to the telephone pole where, according to Crew Cut, the case should be found, but there was no case. More badmouthing resulted, and I had to agree. The guy had obviously split, and the story he gave me did not correspond to reality as well as New Yorker's story. Then Crew Cut appeared, however. He picked up the case near a fence about 60 feet farther from the train than the post where I had looked, and he continued toward us. Such rapid back-pedaling from the vilification just uttered by New Yorker would be hard to imitate. The friendship was reconstructed by New Yorker before Crew Cut reached the train. However, upon an invitation to join his former traveling companion, New Yorker declined. Wheat harvesting was not going to be his line of work. Crew Cut got three pairs of pants and two shirts out of the small case and gave them to New Yorker. The truth was out. New Yorker gave Alex and me each one of the pairs of pants because he did not want to carry them.

The significance of this event may be seen in the broader scope of relationships among tramps. The settings of their lives are ones of relatively constant hustling—hustling for a place to sleep, for food, money, and drink. Sharing seemed to be a norm. Boxcars are another aspect of a tramp's life. With two open doors, each at least eight feet wide, and without safety railings, the number of times one is vulnerable to a quick push to death at many miles per hour with no witnesses is sufficiently large to pre-caution one to travel only with companions one trusts. Irritations are usu-ally shared. Bad feelings are rarely displayed. Relationships are struck up and dissolved easily. The day-to-day-interaction pattern is congenial, unpretentious, and mutually supportive.

After Crew Cut left us, about 10:00 P.M., Alec, New Yorker, and I bedded down for the ride over The Hump, the Continental Divide. With the sleeping bag under us, blanket and canvas over us, Alec on one end, New Yorker in the middle, and me on the other end, we all kept relatively warm with frequent tugging on the ends of the covers and arrived in Spokane some time late the next morning.

I had decided to get off in Spokane, see a friend there, and travel to Pullman, Washington, to Washington State University the following morn-ing. Had I gone directly to Seattle, I would have lost two days to good use over the weekend. Recall that I only collected data on weekday afternoons in early August.

The others temporarily got off the train while it lay over in Spokane. No porters were on hand to assist us into waiting cabs, so with our grips we proceeded directly to a bridge at the east end of the switchyard, about five miles from downtown Spokane. Already in various activities were about ten men as we approached. One unpleasant sort of fellow seemed to check us out. A few were reading. A fire was burning, and we drank coffee from small charred cans and ate vegetables heated in another larger one. Dessert was the scooped-out, salvageable remains of three packages of freezer cookies, wrapped in an old TV-dinner tray and charred without even removing the plastic.

Not much later, we walked four blocks to a small neighborhood grocery store and bought cigarettes, milk, and nuts. Back under the bridge, talk of available work and of how far it was to downtown Spokane and the facilities there led Alec and New Yorker to conclude that Wenatchee would be their destination. We parted with well wishes. One-hundred-fifty yards away I discovered I had left my knife where I had used it to cut potatoes. Halfway back I met Alec and another man. They said they were on the way to the store and had planned, if they saw me, to give me my knife. I thanked them and walked as far as the store with them.

In Spokane I walked to a gas station and looked up my friend's address and phone number but found no one home. I began hitchhiking downtown and caught a ride. I decided to wait until after working hours to call my friend again. I went to a mission in downtown Spokane to clean up and maybe get something to eat. I thought that if I did not reach my friend, I would probably stay overnight. Upon arriving at the mission, I was spoken to as if I were scum, stupid, and sinful. It was a shock after the very pleasant relationships I had maintained for the past three days. I was told that the service was at 7:30, after which a meal would be served. Then I would be assigned a bunk and could clean up. I washed my face and hair in the men's room, then collapsed wearily in the mission reading room with a copy of *Popular Science*. One of the mission employees who had spoken so insultingly to me earlier brought a dish of ice cream and cake and two packages of cellophane-wrapped cookies. He might have seen me help myself to the box of apricots on a counter in the room. I reached my friend about 6:00 P.M., we had dinner and talked, and I did not have to stay at the mission. Showering felt soothingly good after three days of wind, dust, and exposure.

I hitchhiked to Pullman the next morning, conducted the business I could with the people who were there, enjoyed friends' company, and prepared to leave for Seattle. Hitchhiking from Pullman to Seattle on Sunday is a low-probability proposition. A ride was finally offered to Spokane. I took it, thinking it would be easier to hitchhike on the freeway from Spokane, but, incredibly, I stood beside the freeway on-ramp with my Seattle sign from 11:30 A.M. until 6:30 P.M. While standing there I watched two westbound freights pull out with guys standing in the doorways of empty boxcars on both trains. After each train left, I reasoned that it would be a long time until another one. After seven hours of waiting, however, I realized that I might be there until morning and conceivably until the next night. I went to a nearby phone booth and called the Burlington Northern office to enquire if any more Seattle-bound freights were leaving that evening. A secretary transferred my call to someone who wanted to know why I was asking. I told him I wanted to catch a ride. He told me that was illegal but that I should check with the yardmaster. I might have known it was a waste of time to call.

I hoisted my pack to my back and headed down the tracks. As I walked along I looked up to see another westbound coming toward me, too fast to jump, and saw more guys in more empties. I continued, committed in action and attitude to the freights, disgusted with hitchhiking. From downtown Spokane I caught a switch engine pulling a string of cars out to the big switchyard east of Spokane. Asking at the yard office, I found that the next westbound to Seattle would leave early in the morning. Hungry and sweaty, I dumped my pack near the side of the yard office, changed clothes, and began to eat. As I was putting on another sweatshirt, a car drove up beside me and parked in front of a sign that read, "Special Agent." Two men got out, and as they walked past me one of them told me to move to the other side of the yard when I was finished. I moved to the other side and got a good night's sleep. The westbound had no empties, and so I rode a gondola containing some massive electrical-generator parts that arrived in Seattle early in the afternoon.

I checked in at the Yesler Hotel ($3.00 per night, up from $2.25 three years before) and began my data collection. I had checked at two missions first but could not get a room even for pay, only a bunk, and since I had material I wanted secure, I opted for the hotel. The accommodations there were probably not much better, though. Actually, the Yesler is not all that bad a hotel. The bed was comfortable and the one shower on the floor worked well. There were two big metal garbage cans at the head of the stairs on each floor, but the lace curtains in the halls were hopelessly disintegrated, in shreds from top to bottom, and the carpets were faded or threadbare. These things were insignificant. It did irritate me, however, that I could not write a check for the room and had to use my scarce cash.

Taking a break from doing my counting near the Pike Street Market in Seattle, I was tapped for spare change by a man about 50 years old who, after I identified myself as a fellow rail traveler, identified himself as Little Whitey (in contrast to Big Whitey, another tramp who was a bully and picked fights). He told me that the Interbay Yards in Seattle were "hot." One drunk had been decapitated after stumbling on the tracks, and another, also drunk, had fallen under the wheels of a moving train and had lost his legs. The "bulls" were throwing everyone out of the yard, not allowing anyone to ride. Another yard north of Seattle, the Troy yard, had a new young "bull" that was not even so courteous as that. A first sighting in the yard got one jailed. He said it was not unusual for a yard to get "hot" following some sort of incident or another. This period would last up to six months and then things would usually be as before.

I told little Whitey of another, milder case of a "hot yard." Back in Minot, Crew Cut, New Yorker, Alec, and I were going to go into the basement of the tower building to get water but were told not to. We were informed that someone just the day before had stolen the lunch of one of the office people and that tramps were not allowed in the building anymore. Later, a brakey said the railroad people had pulled all the tramps off the train searching for the lunch. Crew Cut had said that when the tower in Minot was new, tramps had been welcome in the basement of the building where hot cans of soup could be purchased from vending machines. In the winter the railroad people would even come and announce when trains were leaving, or so the story went.

On four or five occasions, at least, stories were told of tramps' abusing gratuities and thereby ruining things for others. For example, one monastery that produced sausages was a regular stop for tramps, according to Alec, until the donors once found quantities of their handouts discarded by the railroad tracks with single bites taken out of each article. A certain bakery had also halted its charitable practices when a quantity of its produce was found discarded. Another establishment quit giving handouts because the female manager had been verbally assaulted by a tramp. The norm was clear: Alienating a support source made it tough on everyone so be pleasant and at least appear virtuous.

Having completed work in Seattle, I hitchhiked to Tacoma with less than a ten-minute wait beside the freeway. I walked the Tacoma Skid Row with my pack on my back. I finished around 5:00 P.M. and was walking toward the Tacoma switchyard when I saw at the Town Pump Tavern an advertisement for a foosball tournament that very evening. I knew how to play foosball and decided I needed a break. I had my supper out of my pack and a few beers while waiting for the tournament to get organized.

I drew the one woman in the tournament as a partner. As it turned out, she was not present but was supposed to show up soon. I ended up with a female employee of the tavern as a partner. She was not a very good player so I left after our first match. I was more suspicious that the draw for partners had been rigged against the one outsider in this $6.00 first-place-money tournament than about tramps' stealing my pack.

Around 9:00 P.M. I made it to the Tacoma switchyard, which I had spotted when riding in. I caught a ride almost immediately to the Auburn switchyard, halfway between Tacoma and Seattle, where big eastbound trains are made up. As I approached the yard office to enquire about an eastbound, a man with a signal light outside told me harshly to get back around to the other side of the building, threatening that the "local bull" would be interested in seeing me. I think I got between his signal light and a switch engine which is a bad practice. The next eastbound, I found out later, was leaving at about midnight for Pasco. I waited, checking periodically with switchmen.

I finally got the word that the next train in would be the one I wanted. It was going to switch power, get a new caboose, and then head east. It came past me and I spotted an empty. I headed for my coach but the train backed up. I turned around and walked the other way. Again the train reversed. This time I was not going to miss. For the first time I caught one "on the fly"—I grabbed the hanging door latch and swung in. The train did more switching and finally hooked on a caboose right behind my car. That did not seem exactly correct, but I was tired and thought I would just hope. However, when pulling out of the yard, we did not seem to be heading east. The yard ran north and south so I thought maybe the train went north before it caught the main line east. It was too late to worry about it at that point—I was exhausted. It must have been 1:30 A.M. when I unrolled my pack and slept.

The next thing I knew, the car was stopped and an engine was on the next track, positioned in such a way that the headlight shone right in the door of my car. I looked up and lay back down. Soon came a knocking at the door, and I was being told to get my gear together and get out of there. A few minutes later I jumped down and asked what the trouble was. I was told I was trespassing. We walked about the length of the car. I had never heard what I was doing called that in the past week and a half. I turned and asked where we were and was told the Interbay Yards in Seattle. I had certainly gotten some bad information from two different people. I told the man that I had been trying to get to Pasco, and he then directed me to another train going to Wenatchee. I thanked him and proceeded to settle between the wheels of a semitrailer on a piggyback car. No more than ten minutes later the train pulled out. I was hoping it was going in the right direction. I only knew it was when we entered, and stayed in, the seven-and-one-half-mile long tunnel (second longest in the world), which I remembered from the trip from Wenatchee to Seattle in the other direction. Sharing a long tunnel with four diesel units is not too bad in a boxcar. On that flatbed with semitrailers I curled totally inside my sleeping bag, trying not to breathe. Still exhausted, again I slept and woke up near Wenatchee. It was an uneventful ride to Spokane, windy and dusty under the semi. The piggyback is my least favorite of all the types of cars I rode.

In Spokane, it seemed as if the train was never going to stop. I had forgotten how far from downtown the main switchyard was. I jumped off just before reaching what I thought was the bridge where I had shared food and coffee on the way out. It was the wrong bridge, but it was the one near the gas station from which I had phoned five days earlier. I washed with a soap bar Alec had given me, drank over a quart of water, and filled my canteens. Heading up the track to the switchyard, I asked the engineer in a parked train if he was heading east. He said he was just waiting to get into the yard because his train would be breaking up there but that the train just ahead was a hotshot going all the way to Chicago. I walked on, found a clean, wood-floored car with both doors open and got comfortable. Some switching jerked the car, and then the train sat for over an hour, too long for a hotshot. I got my gear back together. The caboose and a number of cars had been taken off, though the train was still on the main line going east. I enquired at the office and found out it was not a hotshot. It was going to Missoula. The next train to Minot would be leaving that night.

I went to the other side of the yard (I did not need to be told this time) and had some stew with a Spokane native who had just been through a verbal conflagration with his wife and in-laws. He caught a westbound shortly thereafter. Another fellow in a bedroll near the fire got up and took a long pull from a quart of white port. This was the only time on the entire trip I had seen anyone drinking near the tracks. Alec had said that it was crazy to drink while riding. He drank a lot but never near the trains. He said you do not live long when drinking around trains. I talked for a while to an old man, maybe 70, who said he had been riding for a long time, forty some-odd years off and on. He said he had come to the west end of the yard to sleep because there were three colored boys back a way—"They are all right you know, but there are three of them." Another fellow there said he would never sleep under the bridge (the one at the other end of the yard, the one under which I had eaten on the way out) because it is not safe.

I saw fourteen tramps that night in Spokane and talked with six of them. The eastbound came in and I picked an empty. It was a very short, wood-floored boxcar. Possibly because one door was open all the way and the other about 18 inches, it was the windiest boxcar I had ridden in. I rigged up a cardboard lean-to and slept comfortably. The train went through Glacier National Park next morning—spectacular country. Near Glacier the train made a short stop. A fellow in the car next to mine and I watched as two young fellows with backpacks and a dog ran along beside the train for quite a distance as it pulled out. They could have caught one of three gondolas just behind our cars, but not with the dog, so they finally gave up. I wondered what they expected.

I had just two quarts of water to get from Spokane to Minot. I did not think I needed to refill, but two quarts left no excess. When the train made a stop in Havre, Montana, to check wheel bearings and change units (the diesel engines were never called "engines," always "units"), the fellow in the next car jumped out and stuck his bedroll in the tall grass beside the track. He began to dump out his plastic gallon water jug. I knew there was a water faucet in the yard, but I did not know exactly where, and I was not prepared to go looking for it. I yelled at him and held out my canteen. He brought his jug and filled my canteen. When he returned with his jug full and had replaced his bedroll in his car, we talked for a few minutes.

The next morning when the train pulled into Minot, I was just waking up and did not know where we were. I saw a stadium go by and thought it might be Dickinson, North Dakota, because I knew there was a college there. When the train passed the three-story tower at the end of the switchyard, I knew we were in Minot. I quickly began getting my pack together. Before I was finished, my buddy from the next car came up to the open door. He said he was making sure I did not sleep through Minot. I said I had been asleep just outside Minot and that I had at first thought we were in Dickinson because we passed a stadium. He said that the old Great Northern track is the one that goes by the stadium in Dickinson. He was going to somewhere in Iowa, but he was going to Minneapolis first. He decided that he would ride to Grand Forks with me and calculated that by going to Grand Forks, then to Fargo, then to some other point, and then to Minneapolis he would save himself a six-mile walk. The trip through Grand Forks would take at least another day but would end in a yard right in Minneapolis. The hotshot from Minot to Willmar and then Minneapolis would pull into a yard five miles out of Minneapolis.

We found out which track the Devils Lake–Grand Forks–Duluth–Superior train was making up on and looked it over. The choice was between a dirty gondola, with a bottom that drops out to dump a cargo of rocks or something, and a lumber car with about six feet of space at the rear of the car. My buddy did not like the gondola because he did not trust the chains that held the bottom up so we tied our packs onto the lumber car and waited.

We had asked two different men about this train. The first had said that another would not be going that way for two more days. The second said it was not going out until the next day. The first man had just come out of the yard office with a clipboard in his hand and the second was a yardman, but they both agreed that the same train on the same track was going to Grand Forks. We had been waiting about an hour when a switch engine moved the train from about the middle of the yard to the very end of the yard. Apparently the train was not all made up. We walked to the yard office and asked again. There were going to be more cars added, and it would be going out in the afternoon. My friend asked about other trains and decided on one that would be leaving soon that would get him close enough to where he wanted to go. At 3:00 P.M., at 6:00 P.M., and again at 9:00 P.M., I walked to the yard office to enquire about departure time. All they said was soon, soon. At 9:00 P.M. they said it would be leaving right away, that they were checking it right now.

I hurried back and talked to the brakeman. He suggested not riding on the lumber car because lumber is shifty. He thought the gondola would be safer. I agreed and took the gondola.

Having waited twelve hours, through a rainstorm, I had collected a fair amount of cardboard. Cardboard is one of the reasons tramps do not have to carry much baggage. With minimal searching, it is usually available in any switchyard. It can be used for an umbrella, a mattress, a windbreak, a pillow, a shelter, or fuel, though wood is also usually available. Both the available wood and the cardboard come, I suppose, from the packing and bracing of various cargoes hauled on trains. The quality of tramp life would clearly go down if a substitute for cardboard were invented. I made a very comfortable spot in the gondola, with cardboard and part of a wooden packing crate protecting me from the dropout bottom. My only danger would be in sleeping right through Grand Forks.

The train stopped often, and I could not tell what for. The freights I had been on usually had stopped regularly to let passenger trains and other freights by. This time, however, nothing had passed us in five or six stops. I got up each time so as not to miss Grand Forks. (I figured later that these stops were to drop off and pick up cars because this was not a hotshot.) The last time we stopped was near a fair-sized town. Judging by the moon, I thought it must be 3:00 A.M., and given the speed we had been traveling—slow—I guessed we were in Devils Lake. The engines came by on a siding, heading toward the rear of the train. I remember thinking before going back to sleep that they were using one heck of a lot of diesel fuel to pick up someone in the caboose for a coffee break. Later, I woke up with the sun high in the sky. We were in the same place we had stopped—the train had not moved. I spent my last $1.20 on breakfast in a café, got out my hitchhiking signs painted with "GRAND FORKS," and walked through the damp grass to U.S. 2 and toward Devils Lake. I considered going back to the switch-yard but figured that since it was Sunday and the train had been so erratic, it was unlikely that it would be moving soon. Then I heard the deep, lovely sound of the train whistle. I decided that I would check on my train. As I walked toward the tracks I saw three cars painted with the familiar "FRISCO." I had seen those cars moving eastward once before. I covered the 300 yards to the tracks before one-quarter of the train had passed and jumped onto a grain car with a platform at the end. With two cups of coffee moving into my bloodstream, relief at not having to hitchhike, and a wide open view and wind in my face, I was ecstatic.

The 90 miles from Devils Lake to Grand Forks were the slowest moving 90 miles of the entire trip. Apparently, being a day late and traveling on Sunday, the crew was in no hurry. Roughly counting off seconds at an odometer check on U.S. 2, which runs parallel to the track, I estimated we were traveling at 30 miles per hour. Slowing the trip even more were stops at small towns to leave and pick up cars (I could see them in the daylight). Also, for the first time on the trip I saw a hotbox. Smoke poured from a car near the engines. Actually, I did not see the smoke until after the hotbox was repaired. The train had stopped for no reason apparent to me. I got off and was throwing stones into a small lake less than 20 yards away when a man walking on top of the cars toward the engines passed me. I ran the length of the car, and when he stepped to the next car, I asked what the trouble was. He was surprised to see me. He said it was a hotbox but that it would be fixed soon. A half hour later we pulled out, going faster than at any other time between Devils Lake and Grand Forks. For all the smoke that rose then I thought someone was trying to put the car with the hotbox completely out of commission, but the smoke diminished and eventually disappeared. Finally, we pulled into Grand Forks.

Walking into the yard and being greeted by my two screaming daughters and a visiting nephew brought home to me incredibly clearly the nature of the difference between long- and short-term affiliation, between duty and freedom, between continuous security and hustling. The bath that followed my homecoming reeked of luxury in contrast to deprivation, but it erased the reality of a life-style that had welcomed me without qualification. It was sad somehow, but I was returning to a good life as well.

To me, there seems something spiritual about spending one's time in the pursuit of basic necessities. This feeling is in apparent contrast to Maslow's hierarchy-of-needs theory, according to which one does not satisfy the spirituallike human need of self-actualization until one has attained the satisfaction of physical needs, safety needs, affiliation needs, and esteem needs. The apparent contrast disappears when one recognizes the cultural determination of physical needs (beyond air and water) and safety needs. Without a doubt, tramps do not spend all their time in pursuit of basic needs. For example, there are drinking bouts that obliterate all striving. There are hard jobs but comforts as well. The typical nature of the relationship between the tramp and the world may be inferred from the traveling gear of nearly all the tramps I saw. The standard set of possessions is a one-gallon plastic water jug and a small bag—either paper or plastic, occasionally cloth—or a small, hard case containing soap, razor blades, other incidentals, and perhaps a change of clothes.

The stories of the ways in which men begin to "go on the tramp" may to some degree also reflect the tramps' reality. Most often, the stated reasons involve someone's death—usually a wife, often parents, sometimes a lover. The second most frequent reason I heard for leaving a situation to become a tramp involved conflict with wife, in-laws, lover, or a combination of these. I never heard, "So my wife could get AFDC." One fellow said he felt too worthless to do anything else. Usually, however, the self-concepts of the tramps I met seemed as healthy as, or healthier than, most other categories of people with whom I am familiar. This generalization does not apply to men I met in cities on Skid Rows.

I never inquired about reasons for going "on the tramp," but that information was often volunteered. Perhaps that fact in itself reflects a negative self-concept, or it could mean that tramps recognize the low status of their profession and have to justify why they, as intelligent people, would get into such a life. I also never inquired about why men remain "on the tramp." That information was seldom volunteered. Three times I heard men mention that they had been offered permanent employment but had turned it down. The reasons in each case were in terms of affinity for the life of the tramp, the constant mobility, the relations they maintained.

For me, two weeks of break from a desk-ridden summer make the life easy to romanticize. No doubt being a tramp has many miserable moments. I experienced a few. It is an active life—I lost nine pounds in two weeks. It is a life at which one *can* progress in talent and gain relative security. Birds of the air, lilies of the field, and tramps on the Burlington Northern in August are seemingly occupied with few long-term worries; "It's a good life if you don't weaken."—Alec

Appendix A:
Street-Data Limitations

An obvious difficulty in gathering data on sidewalks and parks is the weather, but in cloudy, rainy Seattle, August is the driest month, and only in 1978 was data collection interrupted by rain. No precise temperature observations were made, but sunny days with Seattle's characteristically moderate temperature prevailed every single afternoon of counting except in 1978. One day in 1973 was cloudy and cool until about noon, but then it warmed up.

The rain in 1978 caused 35 to 43 percent of the number of blocks in Belltown, the First Avenue area, and the Pioneer Square area to be missed. International District blocks were 20 percent uncounted in 1978. Pike Street and Tacoma were completely counted, and Fremont and Ballard were not counted at all in 1978. However, the number of blocks missed in each area is not as significant as which blocks were missed. High-scoring blocks were usually covered. Percentages of the 1972 through 1977 counts that appeared in those years on blocks covered in 1978 are shown in table A-1. Adjustments of these magnitudes are made in reporting the 1978 counts in tables 4-2 through 4-8—that is, 1978 figures are increased to compensate for the probable proportion of the counts that are missing rather than the number of blocks that are missing.

The weather in 1978 is a factor of questionable effect. The compensation made for the uncounted blocks is probably a valid move, but the difference in the weather between 1978 and the other years—namely, cloudier and cooler—has an unknown effect on the scores. The 1978 scores are higher overall, and this could be a result of the weather, but if the scores had been lower, one might surmise that this also was because of the cloudy weather. People apparently go outside more in Seattle when it is cloudy. Loiterers in parks contribute the most to the overall 1978 increase.

Human error is another factor requiring discussion. When the data from the first five years, 1972 through 1976, were tabulated together, blocks were discovered to be missing in each year's data: 2 in 1972, 4 in 1973, 8 in 1974, 15 in 1975, and 6 in 1976. The missing blocks were usually peripheral to the high Skid Row-ness blocks, but in some cases rather central blocks were missing from the count. Rather than count these block scores as zero, the average score of the block for years when it was counted was assigned to the block for the year when the count was absent. A slight bias thereby inserted is to smooth out changes slightly from year to year. However, the number of blocks missing, 35 in five years, is not large considering the total number of blocks attempted each year, 189. In all, 3.7 percent of the blocks scored between 1972 and 1976 have estimated scores. A few blocks on the

125

Table A-1
Street-Observation Block Coverage and Skid Row-ness Scores Recorded in the Years 1972 through 1977 on the Blocks Covered in 1978
(percentage)

| | | 1972-1977 Scores on Blocks Covered in 1978 | |
| | 1978 Block | | |
Area	Coverage	Transitory Items	Institutional Items
International District	81	93	88
Pioneer Square area	59	79	82
First Avenue area	65	80	92
Belltown	57	68	92
Tacoma	100	100	100
Pike Street	100	100	100
Fremont	0	0	0
Ballard	0	0	0

periphery were counted only once or twice between 1972 and 1978. They always had close to a zero count and were dropped from comparisons altogether. The count in 1977 was 100 percent complete.

Approximately randomization of time of the week and time within the afternoon data-collection period given to each area over the years probably cancels biases that time-related factors might introduce. This is true especially when considering aggregate data.

One of the indicators of Skid Row-ness—observation of discarded bottles—is complicated by three extraneous factors. First, the City of Seattle hired a person in 1974 to pick up trash, including bottles, mostly in the Skid Row areas observed in this study. His work is apparently evident in the sharp drop recorded that year in the number of discarded bottles observed. Whether funds for the position were allocated the following year is not known, but the count went up again. Second, the city has a regular clean-up crew that works the Skid Row areas in the mornings, thereby depressing the overall count of bottles, especially in the parks and squares. This clean-up operation was not, to the author's knowledge, regular. With aggregate data, again, the variation can reasonably be assumed to level out over the years. The third complicating factor involving discarded bottles is the "Recology Recycling Center," which operated on First Avenue in Belltown in 1974. The operator said that "winos" (his term) brought in bottles. The Belltown count of discarded bottles is somewhat down in 1974. The next year the establishment was called "Belltown Recycling," and the Belltown discarded-bottle count is back up. Perhaps there is some link between these facts and the fact that the recycling center was not in operation in 1976. It remained closed at least through 1979.

Another problematic item in the Skid Row-ness scale is that of loiterers. It would be a matter of uncertain judgment to try to select out those loiterers who are really not "of Skid Row." Non-Skid Row loiterers do make up a substantial number of persons counted as loiterers and included in the additive Skid Row-ness scale. This is especially true in the Pioneer Square area and increasingly so between 1973 and 1978. This is so because between 1973 and 1978, Occidental Square was created and expanded in the Pioneer Square area. The number of loiterers observed from 1972 to 1978 varies up and down, while the number of derelicts observed goes steadily downward. While derelicts are not the only Skid Row people, it is probably safe to say that as the years progressed more non-Skid Row people are included in the loiterer count, and hence, the transitory-item point totals shown in table 4-4 and the number of loiterers shown in table 4-6 are somewhat inflated indicators of Skid Row-ness. It is impossible to say just how much since in all years some loiterers may as easily have been loitering in a suburban shopping center. The loiterers item inserts a bit of invalidity into the Skid Row-ness count, but if an educated guess were to be made, more than 80 percent of the people counted as loiterers in 1977 and 1978 would have been as likely to have been counted in 1972 or 1973 in a Skid Row area.

Reliability questions also arise. Noting transitory items on each block only once per year seems to be, on the surface, an exercise in unreliability. However, the unit of analysis is not a single block but an area. It certainly would be a better study if observations could have been made each day of the year, or each month of the year, but such observations were not possible. Comparisons between the years may be taken as somewhat rough, but the large numbers of items observed each year add at least some credibility to claims that the whole scale is a reliable instrument.

Virtually all of the street-data observations were made by one person, and yearly application of the scale was accomplished with particular effort to uniformly collect data. One other person, a graduate student in sociology, collected data. He accompanied the primary data gatherer and, after many blocks of training to insure reliability, gathered data on about twelve blocks in Belltown in 1976.

In a reliability test in 1978, another sociology graduate student with minimal training in the administration of the Skid Row-ness scale, walked with me and observed, independently administering the scale to the same six blocks I observed. Fourteen of twenty-seven observations of the form, "There were three loiterers between Virginia and Lenora Streets on Western Avenue," or "The Oregon Hotel is on such and such a block," were made exactly the same by both observers. Most of the differences in reporting were minor and resulted from lack of experience in recognizing items on the part of the trainee. However, a few differences occurred because of something the senior observer missed. What this shows is that walking along rapidly with a clipboard, writing names of streets, taverns, and hotels, and making a mark for any of several other items is not a perfectly reliable measurement technique. However, the method appears to have promise. If observers are trained, then consistent, rapid, alert observations should suffice to produce reliable data, certainly reliable for internal comparison, and especially if one researcher makes all the observations. This is true especially if the unit of analysis is large. In this study, the areas examined vary from four to fifty-four blocks.

Appendix B:
Common Names of Areas in Seattle and Corresponding Seattle Police Department and U.S. Census Bureau Numeric Designations

Table B-1
Common Names of Areas in Seattle and Corresponding Seattle Police
Department and U.S. Census Bureau Numeric Designations

Common Name	Seattle Police Department Designation	1970 Census Designation	1960 and 1950 Census Designation
Belltown	124	080	L-0005
First Avenue and part of the CBD	130	081	M-0001
CBD	131	082	M-0002
Upper Pike, just northeast of the CBD	132	083	M-0003
Northeast of Upper Pike area	133	084	M-0004
Southeast of the CBD	134	085	M-0005
Pioneer Square area	064	092	0-0001
International District	151	091	0-0002
South of Pioneer Square area	152	093	0-0003 (part of 093)
Georgetown	180	109	R-0001-A (109 and part of 093)
Ballard	005	104	A-0005 (and part of B-0005)
Fremont	015	049	B-0006

Appendix C:
U.S. Census Bureau Data Sources, Table Names, and Page Numbers

Table C-1
U.S. Census Bureau Data Sources, Table Names, and Page Numbers

Year	Tables	Page Numbers
1952	Table 1. Characteristics of the Population by Census Tract: 1950	7, 9, and 11
1952	Table 2. Age, Marital Status, and Economic Characteristics, by Sex, by Census Tract: 1950	18, 22, 25, and 26
1952	Table 3. Characteristics of Dwelling Units, by Census Tract: 1950	39, 40, 42, and 43
1962	Table P1. General Characteristics of the Population, by Census Tract: 1960	15, 18, 20, and 21
1962	Table P3. Labor Force Characteristics of the Population: 1960	74, 77, 79, and 80
1962	Table H1. Occupancy and Structural Characteristics of Housing Units by Census Tract: 1960	97, 100, 102, 103
1962	Table H2. Year Moved into Unit, Automobiles Available, and Value or Rent of Occupied Unit: 1960	117, 118, 119, and 120
1972	Table P1. General Characteristics of the Population: 1970	P1, P6, P7, P8, P9, and P19
1972	Table P3. Labor Force Characteristics of the Population: 1970	P53, P58, P59, P60, and P61
1972	Table P4. Income Characteristics of the Population: 1970	P79, P84, P85, P86, P87, and P88

Source: U.S. Bureau of the Census, "United States Census of the Population and Housing" Report no. 195 (Seattle, Wash.: Standard Metropolitan Statistical Area, 1972).

References

Alcoholic Treatment Facility Staff. 1974. "Philosophy of nursing care." Mimeographed. Seattle: Alcoholic Treatment Facility.

Allsop, Kenneth. 1967. *Hard Travellin': The Hobo and His History*. New York: New American Library.

Alonso, William. 1971. "The historic and the structural theories of urban form: Their implications for urban renewal." Pp. 437–441 in Larry S. Bourne, ed., *The Internal Structure of the City: Readings on Space and Environment*. New York: Oxford University Press.

Anderson, Martin. 1966. "The federal bulldozer." pp. 491–508 in James Q. Wilson, ed., *Urban Renewal: The Record and the Controversy*. Cambridge, Mass.: MIT Press.

Anderson, Nels. 1923. *The Hobo: The Sociology of the Homeless Man*. Chicago: University of Chicago Press.

———. 1940. *Men on the Move*. Chicago: University of Chicago Press.

Asbury, Herbert. 1950. *The Great Illusion: An Informal History of Prohibition*. Garden City, N.Y.: Doubleday.

Bahr, Howard M. 1967. "The gradual disappearance of skid row." *Social Problems* 15 (Summer):41–45.

———, ed. 1970. *Disaffiliated Men: Essays and Bibliography on Skid Row, Vagrancy, and Outsiders*. Toronto: University of Toronto Press.

———. 1973. *Skid Row: An Introduction to Disaffiliation*. New York: Oxford University Press.

———. 1978. Introduction to *Liquor and Poverty: Skid Row as a Human Condition*, by Leonard U. Blumberg, Thomas F. Shipley, Jr., and Stephen F. Barsky, eds. New Brunswick, N.J.: Publications Division, Rutgers Center of Alcohol Studies.

Bahr, Howard M., and Theodore Caplow. 1974. *Old Men Drunk and Sober*. New York: New York University Press.

Baumahl, Jim. 1973. "I don't have a home and I live there all the time." Pp. 9–30 in Rosenberg Foundation, *Annual Report*. San Francisco.

Baumahl, Jim, and Henry Miller. 1974. *Down and Out in Berkeley*. Berkeley: City of Berkeley and University of California Community Affairs Committee.

Berton, Lee. 1967. "Skid road cleanup: Big cities switch from arresting drunks to try rehabilitation." *Wall Street Journal*, 14 February, p. 1.

Besser, James David. 1975. "The skid row explosion." *The Progressive* 39 (October): 51–53.

Bibby, Reginald W., and Armand L. Mauss. 1974. "Skidders and their servants: Variable goals and functions of the skid road rescue mission." *Journal for the Scientific Study of Religion* 13:421–436.

Black, William. 1926. "Skid Road Rescue Missions." Master's thesis, University of Washington.

Blumberg, Leonard U., Thomas F. Shipley, Jr., and Stephen F. Barsky. 1978. *Liquor and Poverty: Skid Row as a Human Condition.* New Brunswick, N.J.: Publications Division, Rutgers Center of Alcohol Studies.

Blumberg, Leonard U., Thomas E. Shipley, and Joseph O. Moor, Jr. 1971. "The skid row man and the skid row status community." *Quarterly Journal of Studies on Alcohol* 32 (December):912.

Blumberg, Leonard U., Thomas E. Shipley, Jr., and Irving W., Shandler. 1973. *Skid Row and Its Alternatives: Research and Recommendations from Philadelphia.* Philadelphia: Temple University Press.

Bogue, Donald J. 1963. *Skid Row in American Cities.* Chicago: Community and Family Study Center, University of Chicago.

Bowers, Raymond V. 1939. "Ecological patterning of Rochester, New York." *American Sociological Review* 4 (April):180–189.

Brashear, Joy. 1978. "Seattle's success story recycling skid row." *Phoenix Gazette,* 14 June, p. 6A.

Brown, Lawrence A., and Eric G. Moore. 1971. "The intraurban migration process: A perspective." Pp. 200–209 in Larry S. Bourne, ed., *Internal Structure of the City: Readings on Space and Environment.* New York: Oxford University Press.

Burgess, Ernest W. 1929. "Urban areas." Pp. 114–123 in T.V. Smith and L.D. White, eds., *An Experiment in Social Science Research.* Chicago: University of Chicago Press.

Caplow, Theodore. 1970. "The sociologist and the homeless man." Pp. 3–12 in Howard M. Bahr, ed., *Disaffiliated Man: Essays and Bibliography on Skid Row, Vagrancy, and Outsiders.* Toronto: University of Toronto Press.

Chapin, R. Stuart, Jr. 1971. "Selected theories of urban growth and structure." Pp. 141–153 in Larry S. Bourne, ed., *Internal Structure of the City: Readings on Space and Environment.* New York: Oxford University Press.

Churchill, Joseph P. 1976. "Skid Row in Transition." Master's thesis, University of Washington.

Collier, D.F., and S.A. Somfay. 1974. *Ascent from Skid Row: The Bon Accord Community 1967–1973.* Toronto: Addiction Research Foundation of Ontario.

Cooley, Charles H. 1894. *The Theory of Transportation.* Baltimore: Guggenheimer, Weil and Company.

CTSAA (Council of State and Territorial Alcoholism Authorities). 1976. *Report on the Impact Study of the Uniform Alcoholism and Intoxication Treatment Act.* Bloomington, Ind.: Institute for Research in Public Safety.

Dunlap, Riley E., and William R. Catton, Jr. 1978. "Environmental sociology: A framework for analysis." Paper presented at a joint session of the Rural Sociological Society and the Society for the Study of Social Problems at their annual meetings in San Francisco, September 1978, to be published in T. O'Riordan and R.C. d'Arge, eds., *Progress in Resource Management and Environmental Planning,* vol. 1. Chichester, England: John Wiley & Sons.

Fagan, Ronald W., Jr., and Armand L. Mauss. 1978. "Padding the revolving door: An initial assessment of the Uniform Alcoholism and Intoxication Treatment Act in practice." *Social Problems* 26 (December): 232–246.

Faris, R.E.L., and H.W. Dunham. 1939. *Mental Disorders in Urban Areas: An Ecological Study of Schizophrenia and Other Psychoses.* Chicago: University of Chicago Press.

Firey, Walter. 1946. "Ecological considerations in planning for rurban fringes." *American Sociological Review* 2 (August):411–421.

———. 1947. *Land Use in Central Boston.* Boston: Harvard University Press.

Freud, Sigmund. 1930. *Civilization and Its Discontents.* London: Hogarth Press.

Gallant, Donald M., M. Bishop, A. Mouledoux, M. Faulner, A. Birsolara, and W. Swanson. 1973. "The revolving door alcoholic." *Archives of General Psychiatry* 28:633–635.

Greer, Scott. 1965. *Urban Renewal and American Cities.* Indianapolis: Bobbs-Merrill.

Groberg, Robert P. 1966. "Urban renewal realistically reappraised." Pp. 509–531 in James Q. Wilson, ed., *Urban Renewal: The Record and the Controversy.* Cambridge, Mass.: MIT Press.

Guttenberg, Albert Z. 1960. "Urban structure and urban growth." *Journal of American Institute of Planners* 24 (May):104–110.

Harrington, Michael. 1963. *The Other America.* Baltimore: Penguin Books.

Harris, Chauncy D., and Edward L. Ullman. 1945. "The nature of cities." Annals of the American Academy of Political and Social Science 242 (November):7–17. Reprinted in Harold M. Mager and Clyde F. Kohn, eds., *Readings in Urban Geography.* Chicago: University of Chicago Press, 1959, pp. 277–286.

Harris, Sara. 1961. *Skid Row U.S.A.* New York: Tower Publications.

Hawley, Amos. 1950. *Human Ecology.* New York: Ronald Press.

Hawley, Amos, and Vincent P. Rock, eds. 1973. *Segregation in Residential Areas: Papers on Racial and Socio-Economic Factors in Choice of Housing*. Washington, D.C.: National Academy of Sciences.

Hoyt, Homer. 1939. *The Structure and Growth of Residential Neighborhoods in American Cities*. Washington, D.C.: Federal Housing Administration.

Jones, Emrys. 1962. *A Social Geography of Belfast*. London: Oxford University Press.

Kemp, Harry. 1914. *The Cry of Youth*. New York: Mitchell Kennerly.

King County Medical Examiner. 1976. *Annual Report*. Seattle: Division of the King County Medical Examiner, Department of Public Health.

Lee, Barrett A. 1978a. "The disappearance of skid row: Some ecological evidence." Paper presented at the American Sociological Association annual meeting, San Francisco.

———. 1978b. Conversation with author. University of Washington.

Lofland, John. 1971. *Analyzing Social Settings: A Guide to Qualitative Observation and Analysis*. Belmont, Calif.: Wadsworth.

Lynch, Kevin, and Lloyd Rodwin. 1958. "A theory of urban form." *Journal of the American Institute of Planners* 24 (November):201–214.

Manos, Steven S. 1975. "The Manhattan Bowery project." *Alcohol Health and Research World* (Winter):11–15.

Mauss, Armand L. 1975. *Social Problems as Social Movements*. Philadelphia: J.B. Lippincott.

Mauss, Armand L., and Julie Camille Wolfe, eds. 1977. *This Land of Promises*. Philadelphia: J.B. Lippincott.

McCarthy, Raymond G. 1949. *Alcohol and Social Responsibility: A New Educational Approach*. New York: Thomas Y. Crowell and Yale Plan Clinic.

McCook, John J. 1893. "A tramp census and its revelations." *Forum* (August):753–766.

McKensie, R.D. 1921–1922. "The neighborhood: A study of local life in the city of Columbus, Ohio." *American Journal of Sociology* 27:145–168, 344–363, 486–508, 588–610, 780–899.

Meier, Richard L. 1962. *A Communications Theory of Urban Growth*. Cambridge, Mass.: MIT Press.

Montague, Joel B., Jr., and Ronald J. Miller. 1974. "The new professionalism in sociology." Pp. 139–158 in Paul Halmos, ed., The Sociological Review Monograph, no. 20, *Professionalization and Social Change*. Keele, Staffordshire, Wales: The University of Keele.

Morgan, Murray. 1960. *Skid Road: An Informal Portrait of Seattle*. Rev. ed. New York: Ballantine Books.

Murdie, Robert A. 1971. "The social geography of the city: Theoretical and empirical background." Pp. 279–290 in Larry S. Bourne, ed., *The*

Internal Structure of the City: Readings on Space and Environment.
New York: Oxford University Press.

Nascher, I.L. 1909. *The Wretches of Povertyville: A Sociological Study of the Bowery.* Chicago: Joseph J. Lanzit.

Nelson, Howard J. 1971. "The form and structure of cities." Pp. 75–83 in Larry S. Bourne, ed., *The Internal Structure of the City: Readings on Space and Environment.* New York: Oxford University Press.

Newsweek. 1974. "Son of skid row," 23 September, pp. 68, 71.

The New York Times. 1946. "Face lifting along the Bowery includes those on bar-room floors," 11 November, p. 29.

———. 1947. "Proposal to rename Bowery heard again: Something dignified and prosaic wanted," 21 November, p. 29.

———. 1953. "New group will aim to improve Bowery," 30 April, p. 30.

———. 1972. "City's own study urges action in single-room welfare crisis," 22 November, p. 1.

Nimmer, Raymond. 1972. "2,000,000 unnecessary arrests." Proceedings of the Joint Conference on Alcohol Abuse and Alcoholism. Rockville, Maryland: National Institute of Mental Health and National Institute on Alcohol Abuse and Alcoholism, pp. 86–97.

Orwell, George. 1933. *Down and Out in Paris and London.* New York: Harcourt, Brace, Jovanovich (1961 copyright by Sonia Pitt Rivers).

Pastor, Paul A. 1978. "Mobilization of public drunkenness control: A comparison of legal and medical approaches." *Social Problems* 25 (April):373–384.

Pittman, David J., and C. Wayne Gordon. 1958. *The Revolving Door: A Study of the Chronic Police Case Inebriate.* New York: Free Press.

Plaut, Thomas F.A. 1967. *Alcohol Problems: A Report to the Nation by the Cooperative Commission on the Study of Alcoholism.* London: Oxford University Press.

Plunkert, William J. 1961. "Skid row can be eliminated." *Federal Probation* 25 (June):41–44.

Powers, Charles T. 1980. "The hole: Deep under the streets of New York there is another world—a world where the hobos dwell." *Spokesman-Review* 16 February, pp. 13, 14.

Quinn, James A. 1950. *Human Ecology.* New York: Prentice-Hall.

Ratcliff, Richard U. 1949. *Urban Land Economics.* New York: McGraw-Hill.

Ratzel, E. 1897. "Studies in political areas." *American Journal of Sociology* 3 (November):279–313.

———. 1898. "Studies in political areas." *American Journal of Sociology* 3 (January):449–463.

Rice, Stuart A. 1918. "The homeless." *Annals of the American Academy of Political Science* 77 (May):140–153.

Rodwin, Lloyd. 1950. "The theory of residential growth and structure." *Appraisal Journal* (July):101–118.

Roebuck, Janet. 1974. *The Shaping of Urban Society: A History of City Forms and Functions*. New York: Charles Scribner's Sons.

Rooney, James F. 1970. "Societal forces and the unattached male: An historical review." Pp. 13–28 in Howard M. Bahr, ed., *Disaffiliated Man: Essays and Bibliography on Skid Row, Vagrancy, and Outsiders*. Toronto: University of Toronto Press.

Rose, Harold M. 1971. "The development of an urban subsystem: The case of the Negro ghetto." Pp. 316–320 in Larry S. Bourne, ed., *The Internal Structure of the City: Readings on Space and Environment*. New York: Oxford University Press.

Rubington, Earl. 1971. "The changing skid row scene." *Quarterly Journal of Studies on Alcohol* 32:123–135.

Ruppert, Ray. 1972a. "Skid road: People vs. change." *Seattle Times,* 14 May, p. A1.

———. 1972b. "Skid road is changing as church-mission field." *Seattle Times,* 29 July, p. A11.

———. 1979. "Mission going to court to establish its true identity." *Seattle Times,* 12 August, p. C16.

Schmid, Calvin, F., and Stanton E. Schmid. 1972. *Crime in the State of Washington*. Olympia: Law and Justice Planning Office, Washington State Planning and Community Affairs Agency.

Seattle Police Department. 1973. *Statistical Report 1973*. Seattle.

———. 1974. *Statistical Report 1974*. Seattle.

———. 1975. *Statistical Report 1975*. Seattle.

Secter, Bob. 1981. "Hungry, young job seekers swelling skid row in L.A." *Omaha World-Herald,* 20 February, p. 1.

Shandler, Irving W. 1972. "The housing and treatment of the public inebriate." Pp. 49–72 in National Institute of Mental Health and National Institute on Alcohol Abuse and Alcoholism, Proceedings of the Joint Conference on Alcohol Abuse and Alcoholism. Rockville, Maryland.

Shaw, Clifford S. 1929. *Delinquency Areas*. Chicago: University of Chicago Press.

Smith, Wallace F. 1971. "Filtering and neighborhood change." In Larry S. Bourne, ed., *The Internal Structure of the City: Readings on Space and Environment*. New York: Oxford University Press.

Spradley, James P. 1970. *You Owe Yourself a Drunk: An Ethnography of Urban Nomads*. Boston: Little, Brown.

———. 1972. "The moral career of a bum." Pp. 195–217 in William J. Filstead, *Introduction to Deviance: Readings in the Process of Making Deviants*. Chicago: Markham.

Stouffer, Samuel A. 1940. "Intervening opportunities: A theory relating mobility and distance." *American Sociological Review* 5 (December): 845–867.

Suterland, Edwin M., and Harvey J. Locke. 1936. *Twenty Thousand Homeless Men*. Chicago: J.B. Lippincott.

Thrasher, Frederic M. 1927. *The Gang: A Study of 1,313 Gangs in Chicago*. Chicago: University of Chicago Press.

U.S. Census Bureau. 1952. *United States Census of the Population: 1950 Census Tract Statistics, Seattle, Washington, and Adjacent Area*. Vol. 3, ch. 51.

———. 1962. *United States Census of the Population and Housing: 1960 Census Tract Reports, Seattle, Washington, Standard Metropolitan Statistical Area*.

———. 1972. *United States Census of the Population and Housing: 1970 Census Tracts, Seattle-Everett, Washington, Standard Metropolitan Statistical Area*. Report no. 195.

VanderKooi, Ronald. 1973. "The main stem: Skid row revisited." *Society* 10 (September/October):64–71.

Wallace, David A. 1971. "The conceptualizing of urban renewal." Pp. 447–455 in Larry S. Bourne, ed., *The Internal Structure of the City: Readings on Space and Environment*. New York: Oxford University Press.

Wallace, Samuel E. 1965. *Skid Row as a Way of Life*. Totowa, N.J.: Bedminster Press.

Webber, Melvin. 1963. "The urban place and non-place urban realm." Pp. 88–109 in Melvin Webber, ed. *Explorations into Urban Structure*. Philadelphia: University of Philadelphia Press.

Wingo, Lowdon, Jr. 1961. *Transporation and Urban Land*. Washington, D.C.: Resources for the Future.

Wirth, Louis. 1928. *The Ghetto*. Chicago: University of Chicago Press.

Wiseman, Jaqueline P. 1970. *Stations of the Lost: The Treatment of Skid Row Alcoholics*. Englewood Cliffs, N.J.: Prentice-Hall.

Wolfe, Julie Camille. 1977. "Undefeated Derelicts: Skid Row Rehabilitation Potential and Its Correlates." Ph.D. dissertation, Washington State University.

Zorbaugh, Harvey. 1929. *The Gold Coast and the Slum*. Chicago: University of Chicago Press.

Index

Aberdeen, Washington, 62
Accessibility theory, 39
Adult bookstores, 88
Affiliation, 122
Aid to Families with Dependent
  Children, 21
Alcohol, 4; addiction, 101;
  consumption, 2, 3–4, 9–10, 50
Alcoholic treatment facility, 56–57, 61,
  78–80, 90–92, 95, 96, 100, 103
Alcoholic treatment facility staff,
  90–91, 133
Alcoholics, chronic. *See* inebriates,
  chronic
ALEC, 110–115, 116, 118, 123
Allsop, Kenneth, 4, 8, 133
Alonso, William, 40
American Congressional Temperance
  Society, 9
American Temperance Society, 9
Anderson, Martin, 15, 16, 133
Anderson, Nels, 4, 5, 6, 7, 8, 10, 14,
  21, 133
Anthropologists, cultural, 105
Anti-Saloon League, 10
Arrest rates: for drunkenness, 13; of
  Skid Row offenders, 58; for Skid
  Row offenses, 55
Asbury, Herbert, 9, 133
Auburn switchyard, 117

Bahr, Howard M., 4, 5, 6, 13, 14, 15,
  18, 22, 33, 36, 47, 54, 58, 62, 101,
  133, 138
Ballard, 36, 63, 64, 65, 66, 67, 68, 71,
  72, 73, 74, 77, 81, 85, 86, 92, 98,
  125, 126, 129
Barber schools, 2, 53, 63
Barrel houses, 10
Barsky, Stephen F., 58–59, 134
Baumahl, Jim, 102, 133
Begging, 54, 76, 80, 107

Belfast, Ireland, 39
Bellingham, Washington, 62
Belltown, 63, 64, 65, 66, 67, 68, 69,
  70, 71, 72, 73, 74, 77, 79, 82, 83,
  85, 86, 88, 90, 92, 93, 96, 97, 98,
  100, 101, 125, 126, 127, 129
Bentham, Jeremy, 42
Berton, Lee, 16, 133
Besser, James David, 21, 133
Bibby, Reginald W., 33, 134
Big Whitey, 116
Birsolara, A., 135
Bishop, M., 135
Black, William, 3, 134
Blacks, 102, 119
Blood Bank, 53, 63
Blumberg, Leonard U., 3, 4, 6, 18,
  58–59, 101–103, 134
Boeing, 23
Bogue, Donald J., 2, 3, 5, 10, 11, 13,
  14, 41, 42, 47, 134
Bond, posting, 5
Bootleggers, 3
Boston, Massachusetts, 39
Bottle gangs, 58, 63, 74, 107
Bottles, discarded and unbroken, 50,
  107
Bourne, Larry S., 133, 134, 137, 138,
  139
Bowers, Raymond V., 33, 134
Bowery, The, 10, 11, 13, 14, 36
Boxcars, 114, 118
Brakey (brakeman), 112, 117, 120
Brashear, Jay, 24, 134
Bremerton, Washington, 62
Brown, Lawrence A., 35, 36, 44, 45,
  98, 134
Bulls (railroad police), 110, 112
Bureaucracy, 19
Burgess, Ernest W., 33, 34, 35, 39, 40,
  43, 45, 98, 134
Burlesque shows, 2

Burlington Northern Railroad, 108, 115, 123
Business interests, 10
Businessmen, 101

Cafes, 52, 63
Caplow, Theodore, 3, 4, 6, 7, 133, 134
Cardboard, 120–121
Casual labor market, 11
Causal-labor offices, 53–54, 63
Catton, William R., Jr., 28, 135
Census Bureau, data sources, 131; numeric designations, 129
Census data, 56, 61, 82–90, 95, 96
Chapin, R. Stuart, Jr., 37, 38, 41, 134
Chicago Municiple Lodging House, 21
Chicago Illinois, 11, 14, 21, 109, 118
Children, 3
Churchill, Joseph P., 134
Civilization and Its Dicontents, 7
Coffee, 114
Collier/D.F., 10, 134
Communes, 103–104
Communications theory, 38
Con artist, 10
Concentric zone theory, 33–34
Containment of Skid Row, 67
Cooley, Charles H., 37–38, 44, 45, 99, 134
Crew cut, 112–114, 116, 117
Criminals, 3
Cripples, 3
Crookston, city of, 108, 109
CTSAA (Council of State and Territorial Alcoholism Authorities), 20, 135
Cultural area, 33
Cultural ecology, 39–41
Cultural values theories, 39–42

D'Arge, R.C., 135
Death, 114
Degradation, 5
Denver, Colorado, 1
Dependence, 4
Depression, the, 22
Derelicts, 49–50, 63, 70–71, 93, 101, 103, 127

DETOX. *See* Alcoholic Treatment Facility
Detoy Emergency Patrol Van, 92
Devils Lake, city of, 109, 120, 121, 122
Dickinson, city of, 109, 119–120
Dilworth, city of, 109, 110
Disaffiliation, 3, 81, 107
Discarded bottles, 63, 73–74
Distance, linear, 29; ecological, 29; social, 29
Diversion programs, 105
Dominance, 28
Drop-in centers, 103
Drug addiction, 101
Duluth, Minnesota, 109, 120
Dunham, H.W., 33, 135
Dunlap, Riley E., 28, 135

Earthquake, 88
Economic interests, 8
Educational achievement, studies of, 105
Eighteenth Amendment, 10
Einstein, Albert, 61, 105
Emergency shelters, 103
Eminent domain, 15
Empire building, 19–20
Employment agencies, 2
English Coulee (river), 108
Everett, Washington, 62

Fagan, Ronald W., Jr., 17, 18, 20, 42, 55, 56, 91, 135
Fargo, North Dakota, 108, 109, 110, 120
Faris, R.E.L., 33, 135
Faulner, M., 135
Federal Bulldozer, The, 15
Federal Housing Act of 1949, 16, 42
Filstead, William J., 138
Filtering, 34
Fink, 10
Firey, Walter, 39–42, 44, 45, 99, 135
First Avenue area, 63, 64, 65, 66, 67, 68, 69, 71, 72, 73, 74, 75, 77, 79, 80, 83, 86, 88, 90, 92, 93, 125, 126, 129
First Hill area, 81

Foosball tournament, 117
Frank, 110–111
Fremont, 36, 63, 64, 65, 66, 67, 68, 71, 72, 73, 85, 86, 98, 125, 126, 129
Freud, Sigmund, 7, 135
Fugitives, 3
Functional chain, 29

Gallant, Donald M., 18, 135
Gasoline prices, 38
Georgetown area, 87, 89–90, 129
Glacier National Park, 119
Golden rule, the, 42
Gondola car, 110, 116, 120–121
Gordon, C. Wayne, 18, 137
Gradient, 29
Grand Forks, city of, 107–108, 109, 120, 121, 122
Grantsmanship, 19–20, 24
Great Northern Track, 120
Greer, Scott, 15, 135
Groberg, Robert P., 16, 135
Gun moll, 10
Guttenberg, Albert Z., 39, 44, 99, 135

Hager, Harold M., 135
Haight Asbury area, 102
Halmos, Paul, 136
Hamlet, 6
Harrington, Michael, 103, 135
Harris, Chauncy D., 34, 43, 46, 98, 135
Harris, Sara, 5, 135
Harvey, William, 105
Havre, city of, 109, 119
Hawley, Amos, 28, 32–33, 36, 40, 43, 44, 45, 46, 97–98, 135, 136
Health, Department of. *See* Seattle-King County Department of Health
Helotism, 33
Hinterland, 37
Hippies, 1, 85, 102, 112
Hitchhiking, 115–116, 121
Hitler, Adolph, 41
Hobo, The, 6, 7
Hoboes, 3. *See also* Tramps
Hobohemia, 3
Hole, The, 7

Homeless, The, 6
Homelessness, 101
Hotbox, 121
Hot yard, 116
Hotels, 2, 11, 23, 36, 51–52; Missions as, 101
Hotshot, 110, 119
Household size, 82, 84–90
Housing, high income, 40; low income, 21, 37, 44, 99
Hoyt, Homer, 33, 34, 39, 40, 43, 45, 98, 136
Human ecology, 7
Hump, the (the continental divide), 114
Hustling, 114, 122

Impermanence, 4
Independence, 4
Inebriates, chronic, 3
Intensiveness of utilization hypothesis, 30
Interbay yards, 116, 118
Interest groups, 8
International district, 63, 64, 65, 66, 67, 68, 69, 70, 71, 72, 73, 74, 75, 77, 79, 83, 87, 88, 89, 90, 92, 93, 98, 99, 125, 126, 129
International workers of the world, 8
Interviews with Skid Row men, 57, 62, 92, 95, 96
Intracity migration theories, 35–37
Invasion, 36

Jack rollers, 3
Jefferson, Thomas, 42
Jesus people, 112
Jewish Social Service Bureau, 21
Jones, Emrys, 39, 136

Kant, Immanuel, 42
Kemp, Harry, 6, 136
King Count Medical Examiner. *See* Medical examiner
Kohn, Clyde F., 135

Labeling theory, 105
Labor force, men not in, 83–90
Larimer Square, 1

Lee, Barrett A., 14, 22, 35, 40–41, 136
Lenora Street, 127
Little Whitey, 116
Locke, Harvey J., 6, 139
Lofland, John, 47, 136
Loiterers, 63, 70–72, 127; recumbant, 49
Loitering, 76, 80
Lumber car, 120
Lynch, Kevin, 41, 136

McCarthy, Raymond G., 10, 136
McCook, John J., 6, 136
McKensie, R.D., 33, 136
Manhattan Bowery Project, 16
Manhattan East Side Chamber of Commerce, 11
Manos, Steven S., 16, 19, 136
Mariner's Union, 82
Mark, 10
Maslow's hierarchy of needs, 122
Massachusetts, 9
Mauss, Armand L., xi, 8, 17, 18, 20, 33, 42, 55, 56, 91, 95, 134, 135, 136
Median location hypothesis, 30, 32
Medical examiner, King County, 136; records, 58, 61, 81–82, 95, 96
Meier, Richard L., 38, 136
Men on the Move, 6
Military-surplus stores, 88
Miller, Henry, 102, 133
Miller, Ronald J., 104, 136
Milwaukee, Wisconsin, 9, 21
Minimum costs hypothesis, 29, 31
Minimum ecological distance hypothesis, 29–30
Minneapolis, Minnesota, 109, 113, 120
Minot, city of, 109, 110, 111, 112, 119, 120
Mission personnel, 101
Mission stiffs, 5
Missions, Skid Row rescue, 2, 5, 6, 23, 51, 63, 67, 92, 97, 99, 100, 101, 103, 107, 111, 115
Missoula, city of, 109, 119
Model cities program, 19, 24
Montague, Joel B., Jr., 104, 136

Moor, Joseph D., Jr., 4, 101–103
Moore, Eric G., 35, 36, 44, 45, 98, 134
Moral interests, 9
Morgan, Murray, 2, 23, 136
Mouledoux, A., 135
Mount Vernon, Washington, 62
Muggers, 13
Murdie, Robert A., 39, 136

Nascher, I.L., 6, 137
Nation, Carry, 9
National Institute of Mental Health, 24
Natural area, 28, 32–33, 97
Nelson, Howard J., 34–35, 137
New York City, 4, 10
New York City Budget Bureau report, 21
New York Times, 11, 21, 137
New Yorker, 112–114, 116
Newsweek, 22, 137
Niche, 29
Nimmer, Raymond, 11, 12, 17, 18, 41, 137
Northgate area, 81

O'Riordan, T., 135
Observation tower, 112
Occidental Square, 92
Open asylum, 14, 27, 32
Oregon Hotel, 127
Organized crime, 10
Oriental businesses, 88
Orwell, George, 32, 49, 53, 137
Outdoor Cleanliness Association, 11

Panhandling. See Begging
Parasitism, 33
Pasco, city of, 117, 118
Pasteur, Louis, 105
Pastor, Paul A., 13, 137
Pawn shops, 2, 53, 63, 67, 88
Penny arcades, 2, 88
Pensioners, 13
People's Republic of China, 103
Philadelphia, Pennsylvania, 19, 58, 101
Phillips, Bruce (Utah), 1
Piggyback car, 118

Pike Street, 63, 64, 65, 66, 67, 68, 71, 72, 73, 74, 82, 83, 84, 86, 88, 92, 93, 125, 126, 129
Pike Street Market, 116
Pioneer Square area, 63, 64, 65, 66, 67, 68, 69, 70, 71, 72, 73, 74, 75, 77, 78, 79, 80, 82, 83, 84, 85, 87, 88, 89, 90, 92, 93, 96, 98, 99, 100, 125, 126, 127, 129
Pittman, David J., 18, 137
Plasma Collection Center. See Blood bank
Plaut, Thomas F.A., 11, 12, 137
Plunkert, William J., 12, 41, 137
Police: and Skid Row men, 5; and police data, 55–56, 61, 76–81, 95; aggregate, 55, 76–80; individual records, 55–56, 80–81, 98; winter, 76–79
Police department area designations, 129
Police Department, Seattle, 55, 76, 138
Police officers, 101
Position, linear, 29; ecological, 29; social, 29
Potter's Field burials. See Medical-examiner records
Poverty, 3, 101
Powerlessness, 101
Powers, Charles T., 137
Prohibition movement, 9–10
Prostitutes, 3
Puget Sound Hotel, 92
Pullman, city of, 115

Qualitative analysis, 47
Quinn, James A., 28, 30, 32, 43, 45, 97, 137

Railroad police, 110
Railroad tracks, proximity to Skid Row, 54
Rap sheets. See Police Data, individual records
Ratcliff, Richard U., 34, 137
Ratzel, E., 33, 137
Real-estate characteristics, 58

Real-estate interests, 101
Real-estate trends, 58
Recidivism, 18
Recycling, 50, 126–127
Red tape, cutting, 24
Reformist tradition, 6
Reliability, 127–128
Renter-occupied housing, 83–90
Rents, 83–90, 99
Restrooms, 31
Revolving door, 18; padded, 18, 91
Rice, Stuart A., 6, 137
Rock, Vincent P., 40, 136
Rodwin, Lloyd, 36, 41, 136, 138
Roebuck, Janet, 36–37, 44, 45, 46, 99, 138
Romanticism, 7
Rooney, James F., 8, 14, 138
Roosevelt, Franklin D., 41
Rose, Harold M., 36, 44, 45, 98, 138
Rubington, Earl, 14, 138
Ruppert, Ray, 19, 23, 138

Saint Vincent DePaul Society, 82
Salmon Bay Fishermans Terminal, 81
San Francisco, bay area, 102; city of, 102
Satellite Skid Rows, 36, 46, 98
Schmid, Calvin F., 23, 36, 98, 138
Schmid, Stanton E., 23, 36, 98, 138
Scientific interests, 95
Search space, 35–36
Seattle center, 81
Seattle, Washington, 2, 4, 18, 22–25, 50, 52, 53, 95, 100, 101, 104, 108, 109, 110, 112, 116, 117, 118, 126
Seattle police department. See Police Department, Seattle
Seattle, King County Department of Health, 82
Secondhand stores, 2, 51, 63, 67, 111
Secter, Bob, 22, 138
Sector theory, 34
Semitrailer, 118
Service centers, 103
Servicemen, 22
Services required by homeless persons,

12
Sex ratio, 82, 84–90, 102
Shandler, Irving W., 3, 6, 17, 18, 19, 134, 138
Sharing, 114
Shaw, Clifford S., 33, 138
Shipley, Thomas F., 3, 4, 6, 18, 58–59, 101–103, 134
Skid Road, 2, 22–25, 36, 53, 57, 69, 100
Skid Road Community Council, 24–25
Skid Row explosion, 21–22
Skid Row-ness, 104
Skid Row-ness scale, 47–54, 95, 95, 104, 127; application, 54–55; observation areas, 63; observations, 61, 62–76; ratings, 48; grand-total scores, 63–65; high-count blocks, 74–75; institutional items, 48, 65–67; limitations of, 125–128; park blocks, 74–75; periphery blocks, 74–75, 96; primacy of individual items, 69–70; special-category blocks, 63, 74–75; transitory items, 48, 67–74, 96, 98, 104
Slave camps, 112
Slums, 37, 44
Smith, Wallace F., 34, 36, 39, 39–40, 138
Social and Health Services, Washington state Department of, 101
Social engineering, 41–42, 45, 100
Social movements, 8
Social security, 21
Sociologists, ethnographic, 105
Sociology, scientific, 105
Soldiers, 3
Solutions to problem of Skid Row, 103–104
Somfay, S.A., 10, 134
Soup kitchen, 111
Space needle, 81
Special agent, 116
Spokane, Washington, 114–116, 118, 119
Spradley, James P., 5, 9, 138

Stouffer, Samuel A., 35, 44, 45, 98, 138
Street people, 102
Superior, city of, 109, 120
Sutherland, Edwin M., 6, 139
Switchman, 110, 117
Symbiosis, 32–33, 97
Symbol (or cymbal), 108

Tacoma, Washington, 14, 53, 62–63, 64, 65, 66, 67, 68, 69, 70, 71, 72, 73, 74, 76, 109, 117, 125, 126
Tacoma switchyard, 117
Tatoo parlors, 2, 35
Taverns, 2, 11, 52, 63
Tax assessments, 58
Theaters, 54
Thrasher, Frederic M., 33, 139
Time hanging, 9
Town Pump Tavern, 117
Tramp census, 6
Tramp confession, 6
Tramping, 107–123
Tramps, 3, 108, 110, 112, 122, 123
Transportation costs, 31, 99; demand, 37; and rent, 37–38; theory of, 37
Trespassing, 118
Troy Yard, 116
Tucson, Arizona, 4
Tunnel, 118
Twenty Thousand Homeless Men, 6

U.S. Census Bureau, 139
U.S. highway, 121
Ullman, Edward L., 34, 46, 98, 135
Unclaimed freight stores, 2
Uniform Alcoholism and Intoxication Treatment Act, 17, 18, 20, 91
Union Gospel Mission, 101
University of Chicago, 28
University of North Dakota, 108
University of Washington, 81
Unlawful disposition of liquor, 76, 80
Urban poor, the, 102
Urban renewal, 15–16, 40, 42

Vagrants, 3, 101, 103

Vancouver, British Columbia, 62
VanderKooi, Ronald, 2, 14, 139
Veterans Hospital, 81
Virginia Street, 127

Wallace, David A., 16, 139
Wallace, Samuel E., 2, 5, 139
Wanderers, 102
Wants of Skid Row men, 31
Washington, D.C., 17
Washington, state of, 107
Washington State University, 55
Water jug, one gallon, 113, 122
Waterfront, 54
Webber, Melvin, 38–39, 139
Wenatchee, city of, 115, 118
West Madison Street, 3
Western Avenue, 127
Willmar, city of, 109, 113, 120
Wilson, James Q., 135
Wine distributors, 24
Wine drinking, 4

Wingo, Lowdon, Jr., 37, 139
Wirth, Louis, 33, 139
Wiseman, Jaqueline F., 2, 3, 5, 13, 15,
    18, 20, 32, 139
Wolfe, Julie Camille, 57, 95, 136, 139
Women, 3, 4, 54, 102, 112; arrested,
    23
Women's Christian Temperance
    Union, 9
Wretches of Povertyville, the, 6

Yard office, 120
Yardman, 120
Yardmaster, 115
Yardmaster's office, 108
Yegg, 10
Yesler Hotel, 116
Yesler way, 81
Youth, 22, 102

Zone, 28
Zorbaugh, Harvey, 33, 139

About the Author

Ronald J. Miller, assistant professor of sociology at Chadron State College, received the B.A. in sociology from the University of South Dakota, the M.A. in sociology from the University of Toledo, and the Ph.D. in sociology from Washington State University. During his studies at Washington State, he developed an interest in Skid Row people and in the general area of the sociology of street people.